STAAR EOC English I Assessment Secrets

Study Guide
Your Key to Exam Success

STAAR Test Review for the
State of Texas Assessments of
Academic Readiness

Dear Future Exam Success Story:

Congratulations on your purchase of our study guide. Our goal in writing our study guide was to cover the content on the test, as well as provide insight into typical test taking mistakes and how to overcome them.

Standardized tests are a key component of being successful, which only increases the importance of doing well in the high-pressure high-stakes environment of test day. How well you do on this test will have a significant impact on your future- and we have the research and practical advice to help you execute on test day.

The product you're reading now is designed to exploit weaknesses in the test itself, and help you avoid the most common errors test takers frequently make.

How to use this study guide

We don't want to waste your time. Our study guide is fast-paced and fluff-free. We suggest going through it a number of times, as repetition is an important part of learning new information and concepts.

First, read through the study guide completely to get a feel for the content and organization. Read the general success strategies first, and then proceed to the content sections. Each tip has been carefully selected for its effectiveness.

Second, read through the study guide again, and take notes in the margins and highlight those sections where you may have a particular weakness.

Finally, bring the manual with you on test day and study it before the exam begins.

Your success is our success

We would be delighted to hear about your success. Send us an email and tell us your story. Thanks for your business and we wish you continued success-

Sincerely,

Mometrix Test Preparation Team

TABLE OF CONTENTS

Top 15 Test Taking Tips

1. Know the test directions, duration, topics, question types, how many questions
2. Setup a flexible study schedule at least 3-4 weeks before test day
3. Study during the time of day you are most alert, relaxed, and stress free
4. Maximize your learning style; visual learner use visual study aids, auditory learner use auditory study aids
5. Focus on your weakest knowledge base
6. Find a study partner to review with and help clarify questions
7. Practice, practice, practice
8. Get a good night's sleep; don't try to cram the night before the test
9. Eat a well balanced meal
10. Wear comfortable, loose fitting, layered clothing; prepare for it to be either cold or hot during the test
11. Eliminate the obviously wrong answer choices, then guess the first remaining choice
12. Pace yourself; don't rush, but keep working and move on if you get stuck
13. Maintain a positive attitude even if the test is going poorly
14. Keep your first answer unless you are positive it is wrong
15. Check your work, don't make a careless mistake

Copyright © Mometrix Media. You have been licensed one copy of this document for personal use only. Any other reproduction or redistribution is strictly prohibited. All rights reserved.

Understanding and Analysis Across Genres

Determining word meaning

Prefixes, suffixes, and root words

Examples: The word *orthography* can be broken down in the following way: *ortho* + *graph* + *y*. The prefix of the word is *ortho*, which means "straight or correct." The root of the word is *graph*, which means "write, draw, or written." The suffix of the word is *y*, which means "state or condition." Also, adding *y* to the end of the word changes the word to a noun. Using this knowledge, an approximate definition of the word *orthography* would be "the state of being written correctly." In fact, the word *orthography* means "writing words using the proper letters." The approximate definition is close to the true definition.

The word *geometric* can be broken down in the following way: *geo* + *metri* + *ic*. The prefix of the word is *geo,* which means "earth." The root of the word is *metri*, which means "measure." The suffix of the word is *ic,* which means "having to do with." Using this knowledge, an approximate definition of the word *geometric* would be "having to do with measuring the earth." In fact, the word *geometric* means "of or relating to the branch of mathematics that has to do with measuring points, lines, and angles." The approximate definition may help you determine the correct definition because you know the word has something to do with measuring.

Context

When you come across an unfamiliar word or phrase when you are reading, you can use context clues to make a guess as to the meaning of the word. Look at the whole sentence that contains the word, not just the words immediately before and after the unfamiliar word. You may even need to use context clues in the paragraph as a whole. Often, you can find a clue in the sentence before or after the one with the unfamiliar word. Context clues can be descriptions, synonyms, antonyms, and definitions. In addition, the tone of the sentence may help you determine the meaning. Once you take a guess at the meaning, reread the sentence replacing the unfamiliar word with your guess. Ask yourself if the sentence makes sense. If it makes sense, continue reading based on your assumption.

Multiple meaning words: Some words are spelled exactly the same but have different meaning in different contexts. You need to use the context of the situation to determine the correct meaning. Often, these words can be used as either a noun or a verb, and their grammatical usage determines the meaning. The word *trip*, for example, could be either a noun or a verb. *Trip* as a noun means "vacation." *Trip* as a verb means "fall over something." Here are two different sentences using *trip* as a noun and a verb.
1. Last year, she went on an amazing *trip* to Santa Fe, New Mexico, with her sister.
2. If you aren't watching where you are going, you might *trip* over a bump in the cement.

The word *degree* has at least three different meanings depending on the situation in which the word is used. 1.) A *degree* is the incremental measurement of temperature. 2.) A *degree* is a title awarded upon graduation. 3.) Finally, *degree* can mean the extent or amount of something. Here are three different sentences using the word *degree*:
1. You probably don't notice a difference when the temperature rises one *degree*.

2. The employer is only willing to hire someone with a college *degree* in mathematics.
3. It was hard to tell the *degree* to which he really cared about the outcome.

Denotation and connotation

Denotation is the literal meaning of a word or the dictionary definition. The denotation of a word is completely objective. Connotation is the meaning of a word that is derived from the literal meaning *plus* the emotions or thoughts that one has about the word based on experiences, memories, feelings, and ideas. The connotation of a word is subjective. That is, it depends on the feelings of the reader and the situation in which it is used. The words *cheap* and *inexpensive* both have the same denotation of "not costing a lot of money." The word *cheap,* however, has the connotation of being "of low quality," whereas the word *inexpensive* does not have that same connotation.

The denotative meaning of a word is the literal meaning. The connotative meaning includes the emotional reaction that a word may evoke. The connotative meaning often takes the denotative meaning a step further due to associations that the reader makes with the word. For example, the denotative meaning of the word *rat* is "a long-tailed rodent." Many people have strong emotions associated with rats, so the connotative meaning may include words like *dirty, sleazy,* and *disgusting.* Using the connotative meaning, you could call a sleazy person a rat even though she is not a long-tailed rodent.

Example
Give the denotative and connotative meanings of the word snake based on the following sentences:
> One of the largest types of snake is the boa constrictor.
> If he weren't such a snake, we could rely on him to tell the truth.

The word *snake* has both a denotative and a connotative meaning. In the first sentence, the word *snake* is used literally as a reptile similar to a lizard but without legs. In the second sentence, the word *snake* is not used to refer to a reptile, but rather to a person. The connotative meaning of the word is being used, rather than the denotative meaning. You can use the context of the sentence to determine the connotative meaning of the word. In this case, snake means "a crafty, unreliable person."

Foreign words and phrases

There are many foreign words and phrases that are used in everyday English. These words are not English, but are written and spoken as if they were. These words have origins in different languages such as Latin and French. A common Latin phrase is *quid pro quo,* which means something for something. For example, "As a quid pro quo, John gave Sam his sandwich for a candy bar." A common French phrase is *bon appétit*, which is another way of saying enjoy your meal. For example, when the waitress delivered the food she told the couple, "bon appétit."

Dictionary and glossary

A dictionary is a separate reference book with definitions of words in the English language as well as pronunciation and etymological information. A glossary is a list of terms and their definitions that can be found at the back of some types of books, like textbooks and reference books. Dictionaries and glossaries both give definitions of words. A glossary does not have definitions of all words, like a dictionary, but rather a glossary gives only definitions for the important terms in the book, which are either uncommon or newly introduced. A glossary may be used when reading a book about economics, for example, to help define technical terms, or it may be used when reading a chapter in a science textbook.

Thesaurus

A thesaurus is a tool that has synonyms of words. For example, if you look up the word *happy* in a thesaurus, you would see the words *content, pleased, glad, joyful*, and *delighted*. A thesaurus does not give a definition like a dictionary does, but you can use a thesaurus to help figure out the meaning of an unfamiliar word. If you are familiar with some of the synonyms of the word, you can determine a precise meaning of the unfamiliar word. For example, if you looked up the word *exultant* and saw the synonyms *overjoyed* and *thrilled*, this could lead you to its meaning "extremely happy."

Theme

A theme is the controlling idea of a piece of literature. It is the lesson or moral that underlies the story. You can find the theme by first making sure that you do not confuse theme with plot. Every story has both a plot and a theme. The plot is what the characters do. Themes are about human nature, society, or life in general. Literary texts can have more than one theme. To find a theme, ask yourself: "What is the lesson of the story?" "What is the book's message about life, society, or human nature?"

There are common themes that run throughout literature, but they are explored differently because of differences in plot and characters. The most common themes include:
- man's struggles against society
- man's struggles against nature
- overcoming adversity
- the importance of family/friendship
- man's struggles with faith
- sacrifices bring rewards
- Honesty is the best policy.

Synthesizing a text

Synthesizing is similar to summarizing but it takes it one step further. Synthesizing involves taking the main points of a text and comparing it with existing knowledge to create a new idea, perspective, or way of thinking. Instead of using existing knowledge, synthesizing may instead be done by combining the ideas provided in two or three different texts. The reader must make connections between the texts, determine how the ideas fit together, and gather evidence to support the new perspective.

Text evidence

The term text evidence refers to information that supports a main point or points in a story. Information used as text evidence is precise, descriptive, and factual. A main point is often followed by supporting details that provide evidence to back-up a claim. For example, a

- 4 -

story may include the claim that winter occurs during opposite months in the Northern and Southern hemispheres. Text evidence based on this claim may include countries where winter occurs in opposite months, along with reasons that winter occurs at different times of the year in separate hemispheres (due to the tilt of the Earth as it rotates around the sun).

Inference

An inference is a conclusion that the reader makes using clues in the text. In a work of literature, there are things that the author does not explicitly mention, but rather hints at. The reader needs to connect the dots of these clues to draw a conclusion, or an inference. An inference is different from making a guess because it is based on evidence. The reader uses specific textual evidence to make the inference. For example, an author might mention that a character has a messy room and papers falling out of his binder. The reader can infer that the character is sloppy and disorganized, even though the author does not explicitly state this fact.

<u>Example</u>
Discuss an inference you can make about the character of Pip based on the following excerpt from *Great Expectations* by Charles Dickens:
> "I never had one hour's happiness in her society, and yet my mind all round the four-and-twenty hours was harping on the happiness of having her with me unto death."

To make an inference, the reader must use clues from the passage to come to a conclusion. This excerpt tells of Pip, who is thinking about a romantic relationship with a woman. The words "yet my mind all round the four-and-twenty hours" and "harping" lead the reader to infer that he has a crush on this woman and cannot get her out of his thoughts. Pip has never enjoyed her company, yet he dreams of their happiness together. From this, the reader can infer that Pip is being unrealistic about romantic relationships.

Understanding and Analysis of Literary Texts

Classical and traditional literature

When some scholars talk about classical literature, they are referring to literature that has endured through the centuries because of its quality and impact. Shakespeare's plays, Dickinson's poems, and Hemingway's novels are all considered classical literature. The term *classical* can also be used to refer to the literature from a specific time period, commonly that of the Greek and Roman world between 1000 BC and 400 AD. Traditional literature is literature that consists of stories that were passed down through generations orally and were only written down at a much later date. These include myths, fables, epics, ballads, legends, fairy tales, and many other historically oral stories.

Figurative language

Figurative language is language that goes beyond the literal meaning of the words. Descriptive language that evokes imagery in the reader's mind is one type of figurative language. Exaggeration is also one type of figurative language. Also, when you compare two things, you are using figurative language. Similes and metaphors are ways of comparing things, and both are types of figurative language commonly found in poetry. An example of figurative language (a simile in this case) is: The child howled like a coyote when her mother told her to pick up the toys. In this example, the child's howling is compared to that of a coyote. Figurative language is descriptive in nature and helps the reader understand the sound being made in this sentence.

Historical context

Historical context influences literature in a number of ways. The style of the author's writing can be impacted by the historical period during which it was written (e.g., Dickens wrote at a time when authors were paid by the word; this is why his novels are so long). Obviously, the setting of the book includes its historical context. In addition, dialect may be a function of the historical period of the book. When a reader understands the historical context of a particular book, he or she can have a deeper understanding of the novel. Knowing about the time period in which the author wrote, as well as the time period discussed in the novel, helps the reader understand some of the author's choices, including character motivations.

Example

Slavery used to be the norm in Southern states. One of the major ways in which the historical context of slavery impacted literature coming out of the South was the birth of the slave narrative. Slaves wanted to have their experiences documented. After the Civil War, former slaves wrote their stories. These slave narratives have given historians valuable firsthand accounts of life in the South. From a literary perspective, slave narratives are one of the most important genres of African-American writing. Slavery influenced literature by delving into themes of power, racial injustice, and equality. Literature from this time period can help the reader better understand the perspectives and experiences of the slaves themselves, as well as the slave holders.

Effect of sound on poetry

Poets choose words for their meaning as well as their sound. This is because poetry is meant to be read aloud. Sound is an important aspect of poetry. There are two main poetic techniques that take advantage of the sounds that words make. Onomatopoeia is the use of a word that imitates a sound. The words *buzz*, *beep*, and *splat* are all examples of onomatopoeia. Alliteration is when poets use three or more words in a row with the same sound at the beginning. An example is "Boys being boisterous." Both of these techniques have an effect on the meaning of poetry. Onomatopoeia helps the reader hear what is actually happening, while alliteration emphasizes certain words in the poem for the reader.

Monologue, soliloquy, and dramatic irony

A monologue occurs when a character speaks his thoughts, addressing either another character or the audience. A soliloquy is similar to a monologue, but differs in that no characters but the speaker is involved. In a soliloquy, the character addresses his thoughts either to himself or to the audience. Dramatic irony occurs when the audience is aware of something that at least one of characters involved in the story is not yet aware of. The character or characters then act on their lack of information or misinformation until they become aware of the truth. Any of these terms may be applied to written texts, in which case the audience is, of course, the reader. In dramatic texts, all of these conventions may be used by the author to create a specific dramatic style.

Irony

Irony is a statement that suggests its opposite. In other words, it is when an author or character says one thing but means another. For example, imagine a man walks in his front door, covered in mud and in tattered clothes. His wife asks him, "How was your day?" and he says "Great!" The man's comment is an example of irony. As in this example, irony often depends on information the reader obtains elsewhere. There is a fine distinction between irony and sarcasm. Irony is any statement in which the literal meaning is opposite from the intended meaning, while sarcasm is a statement of this type that is also insulting to the person at whom it is directed. A sarcastic statement suggests that the other person is stupid enough to believe an obviously false statement is true. Irony is a bit more subtle than sarcasm.

Dialogue, paradox, and dialect

The terms dialogue, paradox, and dialect all refer to literary writing techniques.

Dialogue is the exact words that a character speaks. In writing, a person's words are put in quotation marks to distinguish the exact words from narration.

Paradox is the use of contradictory statements to create an incongruous situation. Authors use paradox to make the reader pay attention. Often, the two contradictory aspects of the paradox make sense upon further thought.

Dialect is the use of a particular way of speaking a language that is specific to a region or a group. For example, an African-American slave living on a plantation during the time leading up to the Civil War would speak with a different dialect than a lawyer from New

York. Dialect helps root the characters and the story in the setting and the time frame of the book.

Flashback, symbolism, and foreshadowing

Flashback occurs when the author of a story tells the reader events or thoughts that occurred in the past, helping the reader to make sense out of events that are currently happening in the story. Symbolism is when the author uses one object to stand for something else. For example, the author may include a flag flying high throughout a story to show pride in the characters' country and togetherness. Foreshadowing gives the reader hints that an event will occur. For example, the author may indicate that a character feels nervous and is unprepared for a competition, which can tell the reader that the character may not do well when the competition occurs. On the other hand, if the character feels confident and is well-prepared for a competition, the reader can guess that the character will do fairly well in the competition.

Foil

In literature, a foil is a character or element whose purpose for inclusion in the story is to serve as a contrast with another character or element. Usually, the foil will be a character contrasting with the protagonist in order to emphasize specific qualities of the protagonist. A foil may be crafted to varying degrees; at the extreme ends of the spectrum, he may differ from the protagonist in nearly every respect, or he may be nearly identical to the protagonist, except in a single key aspect. Some classic examples of foils are John Watson to Sherlock Holmes or Laertes to Hamlet.

Plotline

Every plotline follows the same stages. You can identify each of these stages in every story that you read. These stages are: the introduction, rising action, conflict, climax, falling action, and the resolution. The introduction tells the reader what the story will be about and sets up the plot. The rising action is what happens that leads up to the conflict. The conflict is some sort of problem that occurs. The climax is the peak of the conflict. The falling action is what happens after the conflict. The resolution is the conclusion and often has the solution to the problem in the conflict. A plotline looks like this:

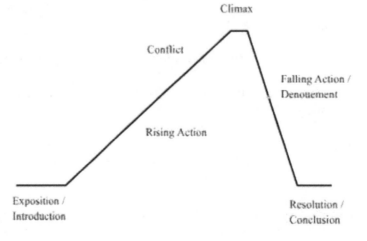

Simile, metaphor, and personification

The terms simile, metaphor, and personification all refer to figurative language.

A simile is a comparison made using the words *like* or *as*. An example of a simile is: She was as fast as lightning as she ran down the track. The author is comparing the runner with lightning using the word *as*.

A metaphor is a comparison of two unlike things. A metaphor is different from a simile because it does not use the words *like* or *as*. An example of a metaphor is: She was lighting running down the track. The author is comparing the runner with lightning but does not use the words *like* or *as*.

Personification is a figure of speech in which an object is given human qualities. An example of personification is: The teapot hummed when the water was boiling. Humming is something that humans do, but here it is attributed to the teapot.

Simile example
Read the following excerpt from "The Raven" by Edgar Allan Poe, identify a simile, and explain what it means:
> Till I scarcely more than muttered "Other friends have flown before—
> On the morrow he [the raven] will leave me, as my hopes have flown before."
> Then the bird said, "Nevermore."

The one simile in the excerpt from "The Raven" by Edgar Allan Poe is: "On the morrow he [the raven] will leave me, *as* my hopes have flown before."
The simile compares the raven's departure with the departure of the narrator's hopes. The narrator is no longer hopeful; his hopes have flown away from him in much the same way that a bird flies away. Thus, the raven's flying is compared to the departure of the narrator's hopes.

Metaphor example
Read the following excerpt from "The Raven" by Edgar Allan Poe, identify the metaphor, and discuss how it impacts the text:
> And the raven, never flitting, still is sitting, still is sitting
> On the pallid bust of Pallas just above my chamber door;
> And his eyes have all the seeming of a demon's that is dreaming

One metaphor in the excerpt from "The Raven" by Edgar Allan Poe is: "And his eyes have all the seeming of a demon's that is dreaming"
The metaphor compares the raven's eyes with that of a demon, thereby, comparing the bird to a demon. This indicates that the speaker thinks there is evil in the bird. The metaphor helps contribute to the overall tone of the poem and the reader's understanding of how the speaker views the bird.

Setting and time frame

Pieces of literature have both a setting and time frame. The setting is the place in which the story is set as a whole. The time frame is the time in which the story is set. This may be a historical period, or it may be that the story is set over the course of one day. Both setting

- 9 -

and time frame are relevant to a text's meaning because they help the reader imagine the story in place and time. Understanding William Golding's *Lord of the Flies,* for example, is dependent upon understanding that the boys are stuck on an island. The setting impacts the plot and the characters' motivations. In the same way, understanding the time frame of the story helps the reader better understand the plot events and historical context of a text.

Visual vs. non-visual texts

Visual and non-visual texts are used to present information in different ways. A visual text will have images such as graphic art, illustrations, or photographs. A newspaper is a good example of this. Most articles in a newspaper have a picture or illustration that goes along with what the article is talking about. On the other hand non-visual texts do not have images to help convey the message. The author must be descriptive in their writing and include sensory details to help paint a picture for the reader. Most fiction is written this way, and also most persuasive and informative texts.

Interpreting visual representations

When you interpret text, you read closely and make conclusions based on the information in the text. The same is true when you interpret a visual representation. You will want to look closely at the visual, ask yourself what it is about, what the tone of it is, why the author made the artistic representation, if there are any symbols, and if there are any instances of persuasion/bias. You will likely have to make inferences because many artistic works are abstract or leave some aspect to the imagination. In many cases, art, to a greater extent than text, evokes a very emotional gut reaction that can be used in your interpretation.

Character analysis

When analyzing a character, you should pay attention to the character's physical traits, thoughts, feelings, attitudes, and motivations. Physical traits include any description of how the character appears. This can include hair and eye color, height, and clothing, for example. The characters thoughts, feelings, and attitudes include his or her ideas about a certain topic or another character. The character's motivations are the reasons why he or she behaves a certain way. For example, in a mystery novel, the protagonist may act in a deceitful way toward a suspect, but the motivation for doing so may be to gain information and uncover the truth. This lets the reader understand that even though the character acts in a deceitful way, he or she is not a bad person, and it allows the reader to better understand the character.

Point of view

The point of view of a text is the perspective from which it is told. Every literary text has a narrator or person who tells the story. The two main points of view that authors use are first person and third person. If a narrator is also the main character, or protagonist, the text is written in first-person point of view. In first person, the author writes with the word *I.* Third-person point of view is probably the most common point of view that authors use. Using third person, authors refer to each character using the words *he* or *she.* In third-person omniscient, the narrator is not a character in the story and tells the story of all of the characters at the same time.

<u>Example</u>
Read the following excerpt from Jane Austen's Emma and discuss the point of view:

> "Doing just what she liked; highly esteeming Miss Taylor's judgments, but directed chiefly by her own. The real evils, indeed, of Emma's situation were the power of having rather too much her own way, and a disposition to think a little too well of herself...."

To determine the point of view, you should first look at the pronouns used in the passage. If the passage has the pronoun "I" it is probably written in first-person point of view. In first-person point of view, the protagonist is the narrator. In the case of this excerpt, a narrator who is not the protagonist is telling the story. The pronouns used are "she" and "her," which are clues that someone is talking about the character rather than the character speaking for herself. This excerpt is written in the third-person point of view. An outside narrator is telling the story *about* Emma. Emma is not telling the story about herself.

Word choice and intended audience

Authors choose words carefully when they are writing. They choose words that precisely express what they want to get across. In addition, word choice impacts the style and tone of a piece of writing. Authors also think about their intended audience when they write. Authors might write the same story differently for different audiences. For example, if an author is writing a story for children, he or she might not include some more disturbing or provocative details that he or she would include when telling the story to adults. Word choice and intended audience impact the text by affecting content, style, and tone.

Formality

In choosing a level of formality in writing, consider the subject and audience carefully. The subject may require a more dignified tone, or perhaps an informal style would be best. The relationship between writer and reader is important in choosing a level of formality. Is the audience one with which you can assume a close relationship, or should a more formal tone prevail? Most student or business writing requires some degree of formality. Informal writing is appropriate for private letters, personal e-mails, and business correspondence between close associates. Vocabulary and language should be relatively simple.
It is important to be consistent in the level of formality in a piece of writing. Shifts in levels of formality can confuse readers and detract from the message of the writing.

Tone and mood

Tone and mood in writing refer to the attitude the author displays toward the subject. Although tone is usually associated with attitude, it may not be identified with the writer. If the language is ambiguous, tone becomes very difficult to ascertain. A common tone in contemporary writing is irony. Tone is communicated by the writer's choice of language. Tone is distinguished from mood, which is the feeling the writing evokes. Tone and mood may often be similar, but they also can be significantly different. Mood often depends on the manner in which words and language are employed by the writer. In a sense, tone and mood are two sides of a coin that color language and enliven the total approach of a writer to the subject. Mood and tone add richness and texture to words, bringing them alive in a deliberate strategy by the writer.

- 11 -

Understanding and Analysis of Informational Texts

Purpose

An author writes with four main purposes: to inform, to entertain, to describe, or to persuade. These purposes play into an author's motivation to craft a text. If the author wants to entertain, he or she may write a novel or short story that has humorous elements and/or dramatic elements. Remember, entertainment does not have to mean comedy or humor; it can just as easily be drama. To determine an author's motives, think about the author's purpose. If the text is fiction, the author's purpose is most likely to entertain or describe. If the text is nonfiction, the author's purpose is most likely to inform. If the text is an editorial or advertisement, the author's purpose is most likely to persuade. Once you identify the author's purpose, you can determine the author's motives.

Summary

The summary tells the main idea of the story, but it doesn't include the details of what happens in the story. It does not include the main characters and what they did or what challenges they faced. It does not summarize the plot. Another problem with the summary is that it is not objective; it is subjective. The writer describes what he thinks about the story. But personal opinions have no place in an objective summary of a story. To improve it, the writer should remove his personal opinion and add descriptions of who was in the story, what important things happened to them, and how the story ended.

Critique

A critique is a detailed analysis of a literary work. A critique is more than just a summary of the work; it also involves the one doing the critique taking a position on the piece, expressing their opinion about the work, and describing what they like and dislike about it. It is a common misconception that a critique is a negative judgment, but many critiques involve a combination of praise and criticism.

Substantiated vs. unsubstantiated opinion

An opinion is a belief, feeling, or judgment that cannot be shown to be absolutely true or false. Even so, not all opinions carry the same weight. An opinion can be either substantiated or unsubstantiated. A substantiated opinion is one that is backed up by facts, examples, expert opinions, or other similar evidence. It is still unproven and still an opinion, but it carries more weight than an opinion without any such evidence. An unsubstantiated opinion by contrast is one that is held without any external evidence to back it up. An example of an unsubstantiated opinion would be, "It is nice and warm outside today." This is an unsubstantiated opinion because it simple states the feeling of speaker. However the speaker could substantiate their opinion by explaining that it is 75°F outside, and include survey data showing that most people believe that 75°F is warm weather. Substantiated or otherwise, it is still an opinion, and another person might still disagree.

- 12 -

Organizational methods to structure text

Authors organize their writing based on the purpose of their text. Common organizational methods that authors use include: cause and effect, compare and contrast, inductive presentation of ideas, deductive presentation of ideas, and chronological order. Cause and effect is used to present the reasons that something happened. Compare and contrast is used to discuss the similarities and differences between two things. Inductive presentation of ideas starts with specific examples and moves to a general conclusion. Deductive presentation of ideas starts with a conclusion and then explains the examples used to arrive at the conclusion. Chronological order presents information in the order that it occurred.

Cause and effect and chronological order

Authors have to organize information logically so the reader can follow what is being said and locate information in the text. Two common organizational structures are cause and effect and chronological order. In cause and effect, an author presents one thing that makes something else happen. For example, if you go to bed very late, you will be tired. The cause is going to bed late. The effect is being tired the next day. When using chronological order, the author presents information in the order that it happened. Biographies are written in chronological order. The subject's birth and childhood are presented first, followed by adult life, and then by events leading up to the person's death.

Compare and contrast example

Read the following thesis statement and discuss the organizational pattern that the author will most likely use:

> Among people who are current on the latest technologies, there is a debate over whether DVD or Blu-ray Disc is a better choice for watching and recording video.

From the thesis statement the reader can assume that the author is most likely going to use a compare and contrast organizational structure. The compare and contrast structure is best used to discuss the similarities and differences of two things. The author mentions two options for watching and recording video: DVD and Blu-ray Disc. During the rest of the essay, the author will most likely describe the two technologies, giving specific examples of how they are similar and different. The author may discuss the pros and cons of each technology.

Chronological example

Read the following thesis statement and discuss the organizational pattern that the author will most likely use:

> Throughout his life, Thomas Edison used his questioning and creative mind to become one of America's greatest inventors.

Based on the thesis statement, the reader can assume that the author is most likely going to use chronological order to organize the information in the rest of the essay. Chronological order presents information in the order that it occurred. It is often used as the organizational structure in biographies as a way to logically present the important events in a person's life. The words "throughout his life" clue in the reader to the chronological organizational structure. The author will probably discuss Edison's childhood and initial inventions first and then move on to his later queries and inventions.

Credible information source

When you find sources for information, whether for a research paper or for your own personal knowledge, it is important to evaluate the credibility of the source. This is especially important to do when finding sources on the Internet because anyone can create a Web page and publish their writing. To determine credibility, look for the author of the information and what that author's credentials are or the organization that is putting out the information. Ask yourself the following questions: "Why is the author or organization publishing this information?" "Do they have an agenda?" "Is the source written in an objective way?" "Is there persuasive language being used?"

Rhetorical schemes

Authors use rhetorical schemes to emphasize, to draw analogies, and to engage the reader. A common technique is parallelism, in which several sentences are given the same grammatical structure in order to highlight the similarities between their content. For example, "Hector went to the store. He went to the bank. He went to the gym." By expressing this information in three very simple statements, the author suggests the dullness of these activities. Another rhetorical scheme is repetition, in which the author uses the same word several times quickly, either to call its meaning into question or to draw emphasis. Consider the sentence "They called him a slave, he thought of himself as a slave, and his prospects were no better than those of a slave." The repetition of the word *slave* mimics the plodding, hopeless nature of slavery, but also causes the reader to focus on the word and consider whether it is really appropriate here.

Procedural texts

Procedural texts tell you how to accomplish a specific task. An example of this type of text is a recipe. The recipe will tell you what ingredients you need and all the information it will take to make the finished product. Another example of a procedural text is an instruction booklet that tells you how to put something together. Often procedural texts are accompanied by charts, diagrams, illustrations and graphs. These things help the reader to understand the information. Charts are used to list ingredients or parts that will be needed for the procedure. Diagrams are very helpful because they use pictures to show you how to complete a certain part of the procedure. Illustrations are helpful because they also can show you how something is supposed to look at steps along the way or a completed project. Graphs can also sometimes be used to show you information about other people's experiences with the same product or procedure.

Inductive and deductive reasoning

Authors use both inductive and deductive reasoning to organize their ideas and structure a piece of text. Inductive reasoning involves making a conclusion based on a specific set of facts. When an author organizes information inductively, he or she presents facts and details and then moves to a general conclusion based on that information. Deductive reasoning, on the other hand, presents the conclusion first and then explains the facts, details, and examples used to arrive at the conclusion. Inductive reasoning is more of a "bottom-up" structure, and deductive reasoning is more of a "top-down" method for presentation of ideas.

- 14 -

Informative texts, entertaining texts, and advertisements

There are four author's purposes: to inform, to describe, to entertain, and to persuade. These purposes apply to written texts as well as media forms. Informative texts are written to inform. Entertaining texts are written to entertain. Advertisements are written to persuade the reader/viewer to believe or do something. You can determine the author's purpose by asking yourself the following question: "Why did the author write this?" An example of an informative media form is a documentary. Entertaining media forms include movies and television shows. Advertisements in media can be commercials or print ads in magazines.

Composition

Composition planning

Before you begin writing, you must spend some time planning what you are going to say. However, you should never assume that you can create a comprehensive outline in advance of a composition, because you will inevitably revise and expand your message during the writing process.

To begin with, consider the basic characteristics of your writing assignment: that is, the topic, length, format, intent, resources, and audience. Some of these characteristics may be undetermined in the beginning. It is important to consider whether your chosen topic can be covered effectively in the required space. A topic may need to be expanded or narrowed in order to fit the assigned length. Also, you should consider whether your topic is appropriate to the writing task and audience. If you are being asked to incorporate external references (i.e., if you are being asked to write a research paper), you should determine whether there will be enough (or too many) references for you to complete your task.

Planning exercises

<u>Listing and freewriting</u>
Often, writers find that the hardest thing about writing is getting started. There are a number of exercises that can help you get "into" your topic during the planning stage. Many writers begin by creating a list of ideas related to the subject. These ideas can be facts, opinions, or even questions. The important thing is to get them down on paper so that they can be examined critically. The mechanical act of composing such a list helps the brain organize itself and chart a path for writing. Some writers make a list on the computer and then rearrange the items until a vague structure emerges. Then, they set to work on a more detailed outline.

Freewriting is another useful planning exercise in which you simply write as fast as you can about your subject until you run out of things to say. A free-write is not expected to be organized or even grammatical. It is just a way to get things down on the page so that they can be evaluated and ordered.

<u>Notes and concept maps</u>
If you are planning a research paper or a response to a piece of writing, you will probably need to take some notes during the planning process. As you read the relevant texts, jot down any crucial ideas or questions that emerge. After you have completed your reading, these notes will be used to form your outline. Your notes tell you what was most interesting, essential, or problematic about the text. You can even make your notes into a list, and then rearrange them into the structure of a response or research paper.

Some writers, especially those with a visual bent, write down the main ideas and terms from the text and arrange them according to their relationships. This diagram is called a concept map. It depicts the general structure of the topic being addressed. Oftentimes, the creation of a concept map helps a writer discover surprising connections.

Outlines

Toward the end of the planning stage, you should construct an outline. The degree of structure and detail in your outline will depend on the nature of the assignment and your work to this point. An outline should mimic the organization of the composition. Its purpose is to order and prioritize the main elements of the piece. The outline should begin with the thesis statement, which is a short summation of the main idea. Underneath the main idea, the most important supporting ideas should be listed. Under each of these, and slightly indented, should be a list of supporting details. These details may also be supported by further information. The various elements of the structure (supporting ideas details, etc.) should be organized with Roman numerals, numbers, and letters. In the most common outline structure, the most general ideas are assigned Roman numerals (I, II, III, etc.), supporting ideas are assigned capital letters (A, B, C, etc.), and even more specific points are identified with numbers. An extremely detailed and complex outline may also need to use lower-case numerals and letters.

Order of sections of a draft

In most pieces of writing, the thesis statement will be in the first paragraph. When composing an initial draft, however, some writers choose to write the body paragraphs before returning to write an initial version of the thesis. This might be a good idea when the thesis is still vague, and you think the process of drafting body paragraphs will help you refine the main idea. When composing with multiple drafts, it is usually best to begin wherever the work appears to be the easiest. As you are completing this work, you will most likely have some insights into how you should handle other areas of the first draft. In any case, tackling the most inviting sections of the draft first helps you make immediate progress, which is a great boost to morale. There is no reason why a first draft, which will be reread and edited several more times, must be written in the order in which it will be read.

Drafting a thesis statement

The thesis statement expresses the main idea of the composition. Every idea, argument, and detail in the composition should relate in some way to the thesis. When drafting the thesis statement, you must take care that you are general enough to include everything that is to follow, but specific enough that you are making a clear point. As much as possible, the thesis statement should be a short, declarative statement that can be evaluated by the reader. A thesis statement should not be a vague, subjective claim ("The Principal is basically a nice guy"); it should be more precise and testable ("The Principal's policies demonstrate his care for students"). The thesis statement should suggest the content of the rest of the piece, so that your audience will know what to expect.

Drafting body paragraphs

Body paragraphs follow the thesis statement. They supply supporting ideas, arguments, and details. When creating a first draft, many writers often start with the body paragraphs, because they are more likely than the thesis or conclusion to be based on manageable facts. In the body of an essay, each paragraph should express a single important supporting idea. This idea should be clear and, in most cases, it should be at the beginning of the paragraph. Sometimes, for dramatic effect, a writer will wait until the end of a paragraph to give the main point. It is also possible that the first sentence of the paragraph will be a transition

- 17 -

from the previous paragraph, and so the main idea will not be expressed until the second sentence. In any case, all of the sentences in a body paragraph should support both the main idea of the paragraph and of the essay as a whole. However, each body paragraph should not merely repeat the thesis statement. Rather, the thesis statement should be developed (expanded and refined) in each successive paragraph.

Drafting conclusions

Writers often find the conclusion paragraph to be the most difficult to draft, because there is an expectation that it should be profound or inspiring. It is true that a conclusion paragraph should avoid simply restating the thesis statement, and that it should suggest some questions or considerations raised by the preceding text, but it does not have to be mystical or even philosophical. A good conclusion paragraph will remind the reader of the initial thesis by suggesting some applications, some questions that have been raised, or some possible counterarguments. The conclusion should indicate how the reader should think about this subject in the future. It should be memorable, because it will be the final impression taken away by the reader. Many writers save a fascinating detail, anecdote, or quote for the conclusion paragraph, where they know it will have maximum impact.

General revision

Once a first draft has been completed, the best thing to do is set it aside for a while. Of course, this is not always possible. Revision is most successful, however, when it is performed with a sense of detachment. In the heat of composition, it is easy to become wedded to ideas and structures that are much less appealing when viewed from a distance. Before you begin revising specific elements of your first draft, look at the document as a whole. Consider whether it truly addresses the intended audience: that is, whether it is written in a style and at a level of complexity that will engage the people you want to impress. You should also think about whether the first draft has the proper organization. You may discover that the argument would be more effective if the body paragraphs were slightly reordered. If you have written a research paper, your general revision should include a survey of citations and references.

Conflict

Conflict is a central element of plot in a piece of literature. The conflict is the struggle or problem around which the plot centers. There are two basic types of conflicts: external conflicts and internal conflicts. External conflicts occur when the main character has a struggle with another force. This may be another character or a force of nature. Internal conflicts are struggles that the main character has within him or herself. For example, when a character has to decide between right and wrong, he or she is dealing with an internal conflict.

Literary tropes

To engage and entertain the reader, many writers will use literary tropes, or figurative language. Some common examples of tropes are metaphors, similes, understatement, and irony. All of these tropes can be employed to good effect, but they must be appropriate to the subject. For instance, a metaphor (a statement in which one thing is described in terms of another – *The moon was a jagged knife*) can be a great way of relating an unfamiliar

- 18 -

subject to something with which the reader is more familiar. However, metaphors have a tendency to become excessively florid and complex, which can distract from the discussion at hand. When dealing with a dry subject, figurative language should be used sparingly. In persuasive and interpretive writing, on the other hand, figurative language can be a great way to establish a tone and engage the imagination of the reader.

The most common literary tropes in student writing are metaphors, similes, analogies, hyperbole, understatement, rhetorical questioning, and irony. A metaphor is a description of one thing in terms of another such as: *Her eyes were pools of crystal blue water*. Obviously her eyes were not literally composed of water, but the metaphor creates an image of cool, peaceful blue eyes. A simile is much the same as a metaphor, but it uses either *like* or *as* (*Her eyes were like pools*), which places a little distance between the object and the figurative representation. Analogies are similar as well, but they compare relationships: *He followed his father like the chicks followed the mother hen*. Hyperbole is overstatement (*Paul Bunyan was as tall as a house*), the opposite of understatement (*Paul Bunyan was pretty tall*). A rhetorical question is posed for effect, not because it will be answered, as in: *How many people must die before we recognize this problem?* Finally, irony is the most complex literary trope. It is the expression by the author of ideas or sentiments that he or she seems to not actually hold. Sarcasm (*The Titanic did a great job of crossing the Atlantic*) is an example of heavy irony.

Final proofreading

After your paper has been fully revised and edited, you should perform a final proofreading. This is a slow, careful check for typographical and grammatical errors. By this point in the writing process, you should be finished evaluating and revising the content and structure of the paper. The final proofread is more targeted at small errors that will distract the reader. At present, the greatest enemy of effective proofreading is the spell-check feature in word-processing programs. Too many students believe that this function saves them the trouble of performing a final proofread. However, spell-checkers are terrible at spotting errors of grammar and diction. If you use the wrong word by accident, your spell-check will never know (unless of course you misspell the incorrect word). Many writers find proofreading to be very dull, but it is vastly preferable to the embarrassment of turning in an essay with obvious mistakes.

Validity, reliability, and relevance of primary and secondary sources

Research papers depend on information taken from primary and secondary sources. A primary source derives directly from the topic, with no intermediation. Examples of primary sources include diaries, eyewitness accounts, videos, letters, legislative documents, and experimental data. Secondary sources, on the other hand, are commentaries or interpretations of primary sources. Some familiar secondary sources include books and articles of history and literary criticism. When incorporating these sources into your writing, be sure that you only use those that are valid, reliable, and relevant. The validity of a source is indicated by the extent to which it is confirmed and echoed in other works. When a source is considered valid, it will be cited in other texts on the same subject. The reliability of a source is the extent to which it consistently supports the point you are using it to make. A work would be unreliable, for instance, if it consistently makes statements only to undermine them later. The relevance of a source is the extent to which it applies to the subject of your essay.

Revision

Revising

When revising a draft, make sure the writing is clear. Look over each paragraph carefully and check to see if something has to be added or taken out. Look to see if an idea has to be supported in more detail. See if rearranging the order of the paragraphs will help the writing make more sense. If a paragraph is too long, perhaps it needs to be cut into two paragraphs. Check for errors in spelling and punctuation as well. The writing should progress easily and naturally. Any ideas that are brought up should have enough support behind them. Reread the draft, make the changes that are needed, and make sure that the purpose of the writing is clear.

Introduction

An introduction announces the main point of the work. It will usually be a paragraph of 50 to 150 words, opening with a few sentences to engage the reader, and concluding with the essay's main point. The sentence stating the main point is called the thesis sentence. If possible, the sentences leading to the thesis should attract the reader's attention with a provocative question, vivid image, description, paradoxical statement, quotation, or anecdote. The thesis sentence could also appear at the beginning of the introduction. Some types of writing do not lend themselves to stating a thesis in one sentence. Personal narratives and some types of business writing may be better served by conveying an overriding purpose of the text, which may or may not be stated directly. The important point is to impress the audience with the rationale for the writing.

Conclusion

The conclusion of a text is typically found in the last one or two paragraphs of the text. A conclusion wraps-up the text and reminds the reader of the main point of the text. The conclusion is the author's way of leaving the reader with a final note to remember about the paper and comes after all the supporting points of the text have been presented. For example, a paper about the importance of avoiding too much sunlight may have a conclusion that reads: By limiting sun exposure to 15 minutes a day and wearing sunscreen of at least SPF 15, a person can reduce their risk of getting skin cancer later in life.

Sentence Structures

The four major types of sentence structure are:

1. Simple sentences: Simple sentences have one independent clause with no subordinate clauses. A simple sentence may contain compound elements—a compound subject, verb, or object, for example—but does not contain more than one full sentence pattern.
2. Compound sentences: Compound sentences are composed of two or more independent clauses with no subordinate clauses. The independent clauses are usually joined with a comma and a coordinating conjunction or with a semicolon.
3. Complex sentences: A complex sentence is composed of one independent clause with one or more dependent clauses.

4. Compound-complex sentences: A compound-complex sentence contains at least two independent clauses and at least one subordinate clause. Sometimes they contain two full sentence patterns that can stand alone. When each independent clause contains a subordinate clause, this makes the sentence both compound and complex.

Transitional words and phrases

A good writer will use transitional words and phrases to guide the reader through the text. You are no doubt familiar with the common transitions, though you may never have considered how they operate. Some transitional phrases (*after, before, during, in the middle of*) give information about time. Some indicate that an example is about to be given (*for example, in fact, for instance*). Writers use them to compare (*also, likewise*) and contrast (*however, but, yet*). Transitional words and phrases can suggest addition (*and, also, furthermore, moreover*) and logical relationships (*if, then, therefore, as a result, since*). Finally, transitional words and phrases can demarcate the steps in a process (*first, second, last*). You should incorporate transitional words and phrases where they will orient your reader and illuminate the structure of your composition.

Persuasive essay

A persuasive essay tries to convince the reader to adopt the viewpoint of the writer on a particular issue. In order for this to work, the essay needs to be on a topic that is susceptible to reason. An essay like "Chocolate ice cream is the best" will never work, because it depends on taste rather than logic. Some people will always prefer vanilla. A better topic for a persuasive essay would be, "Ice cream parlors should come up with more varieties of chocolate ice cream," because this assertion could be supported by market research and cost information. A persuasive essay should always demonstrate a keen understanding of its audience. The writer should consider the interests, prior knowledge, and learning style of the audience when constructing his or her argument.

Thesis

Introductory paragraphs are always important, but they are especially so in persuasive essays, where the author needs to make a strong first impression. In most cases, it is a bad idea to make the first sentence of the essay a thesis statement. Instead, the first few sentences should be used to establish the author's credibility and to win the trust (or at least interest) of the reader. Many persuasive pieces begin with an anecdote or story that introduces the subject in an emotional or narrative context. Once the reader's interest has been piqued, the writer ends the introductory paragraph by delivering the thesis of the argument. An author creates the appearance of credibility by providing essential facts and observations, and by indicating his or her own experience with the issue. Of course, this can be overdone, and the author should avoid looking vain or self-important.

Making claims

A persuasive essay will likely focus on one central argument, but it may make many smaller claims along the way. These are subordinate arguments with which the reader must agree if he or she is going to agree with the central argument. The central argument will only be as strong as the subordinate claims. These claims should be rooted in fact and observation, rather than subjective judgment. The best persuasive essays provide enough supporting detail to justify claims without overwhelming the reader. Remember that a fact must be susceptible to independent verification: that is, it must be something the reader could confirm. Also, statistics are only effective when they take into account possible objections. For instance, a statistic on the number of foreclosed houses would only be useful if it was taken over a defined interval and in a defined area. Most readers are wary of statistics, because they are so often misleading. If possible, a persuasive essay should always include references so that the reader can obtain more information. Of course, this means that the writer's accuracy and fairness may be judged by the inquiring reader.

Examples and expert opinions
A persuasive essay will often use examples to illustrate the main points of its argument, but these examples can as easily undermine the argument if they are chosen and presented improperly. Indeed, examples are most effective when they complement facts. When they are used, examples should be obviously appropriate to the argument. They are a good way to make dry facts and statistics more interesting or comprehensible for the reader.

Expert opinions can also be useful for this purpose, though they must be included with care. The expert should have a title or credential that clearly indicates his or her knowledge and experience in the topic. Also, the quote or reference from the expert should clearly be appropriate to the argument. If the expert quote does not actually support the argument, but is merely recorded to lend an air of sophistication, it should not be included. Also, the source material should always be provided to the reader.

Emotional appeals
Opinions are formed by emotion as well as reason, and persuasive writers often appeal to the feelings of the reader. Although readers should always be skeptical of this technique, it is often used in a proper and ethical manner. For instance, there are many subjects that have an obvious emotional component, and therefore cannot be completely treated without an appeal to the emotions. Consider an article on drunk driving: it makes sense to include some specific examples that will alarm or sadden the reader. After all, drunk driving often has serious and tragic consequences. Emotional appeals are not appropriate, however, when they attempt to mislead the reader. For instance, in political advertisements it is common to emphasize the patriotism of the preferred candidate, because this will encourage the audience to link their own positive feelings about the country with their opinion of the candidate. However, these ads often imply that the other candidate is unpatriotic, which in most cases is far from the truth. Another common and improper emotional appeal is the use of loaded language, as for instance referring to an avidly religious person as a "fanatic" or a passionate environmentalist as a "tree hugger." These terms introduce an emotional component that detracts from the argument.

Persuasive techniques

Glittering generalities
The persuasive technique of glittering generalities means using words that sound great but do not convey much meaning. The words, phrases, or slogans may sound nice, but they are vague. When an author uses glittering generalities, he or she is trying to appeal to the reader or listener's emotions without making any promises. Authors appeal to a reader or listener's sense of love, respect, patriotism, or freedom, among other things. One example of glittering generalities can be in a political speech. The speaker appeals to the listener's sense of emotions to garner support but will carefully not make any promises.

<u>Logical fallacies</u>
The persuasive technique of logical fallacies is using common errors in reasoning to persuade someone of something. Two types of logical fallacies are slippery slope and hasty generalizations. In slippery slope, you say that if something happens it automatically means that something else will happen, even though this may not be true. An example of slippery slope would be to say that if a little shampoo gets your hair clean, a lot of shampoo would get it cleaner. This is not the case. Once your hair is clean, it cannot get any cleaner. Hasty generalization is drawing a conclusion too early. An example of a hasty generalization would be to say, "Even though I have only used this product for one day, I know it is going to change my life by saving me so much time."

<u>Example</u>
Read the wording from a flier advertising an event and discuss which persuasive technique is being used:

> Come one, come all to the greatest event of the year. If you love your school, come on out to join in the fun and excitement! Join us to help make your school a better place!

The persuasive technique being used on the flier advertising a school-wide event is that of glittering generalities. The tone of the wording and the use of exclamation points makes the event sound fun and appeals to the reader's love of the school, but the advertisement contains no specific information about what the event actually is. What will people be doing at this event that will be fun and will make the school a better place? There is no actual meaning to these words because the reader does not know what the event is, but it does appeal to the reader's emotions.

Editing

Editing

Editing has many purposes. One important purpose is to make sure that standard English is being used. This means checking to see if the verb tenses are correct and if the verbs agree with their subject. This also means checking for other grammatical mistakes including the correct use of punctuation and spelling. Pronouns need to be checked so the correct form is used and pronoun antecedents or referents must be checked to see if they agree with each other. Another main purpose of editing is to ensure that there are varied sentences used and that the writing flows from one idea to another. Again, an editor would look for the appropriate word choices to make the writing more specific and engaging.

Gerunds, infinitives, and participles

Gerunds, infinitives, and participles are all verb forms.
Gerund – A verb ending in -ing that is used as a noun in a sentence. Example: We admired the vocalist's singing.

Infinitive – A singular verb preceded by the word to which is considered the base form, or unconjugated form, of a verb. Example: She loves to sing.

Participle – Participles end in -ing like gerunds and form the progressive tense of the verb. Example: The sleeping baby is snoring.

Demonstrative, reflexive, intensive, and reciprocal pronouns

Demonstrative pronouns (this/these, that/those) indicate distance.
This/these usually indicate nearness in time or space.
That/those usually indicate more distant time and space.
This/that are used with singular nouns.
These/those are used with plural nouns.

When the exact quantity or identity of a person, idea or thing, is unknown, use an indefinite pronoun. Although most indefinite pronouns take singular verbs, a few indefinite pronouns take plural verbs and some can take either singular or plural.
Singular Verb: anybody, everyone, something
Plural Verb: few, many, several
Singular/Plural: most, some

Intensive/reflexive pronouns are made by adding -self, -selves to personal pronouns. For example: myself, ourselves. An intensive pronoun emphasizes the noun or pronoun that comes before it. Example: Doug did the work himself.

A reflexive pronoun indicates that the subject and the object of an action are the same person. Example: Ed shot himself in the foot.

Reciprocal pronouns are each other, one another. They refer back to a compound or a plural subject to indicate a relationship.

Restrictive and nonrestrictive clauses

A restrictive clause is a clause that is necessary to make a sentence specific enough to be understood. They are typically used in combination with more general descriptions to identify a specific person or thing. A nonrestrictive clause is a clause that gives additional information about the person or thing being discussed, but is not necessary to identify that person or thing. Restrictive clauses usually begin with one of the relative pronouns *who* or *that*, and are not set off with commas. Nonrestrictive clauses usually begin with either *who* or *which*, and are set off with commas.

Restrictive clause example
I am friends with the kid that lives next door.

In this sentence, "that lives next door" is a restrictive clause. It defines who the friend is. The friend cannot be identified without this clause.

Nonrestrictive clause example
I am friends with Tommy, who lives next door.

In this sentence, "who lives next door" is a nonrestrictive clause. It does not define who the friend is; it merely gives extra information about the friend.

Conventions of written English

The conventions of written language include using capitalization and punctuation correctly. Proper names, the first word of sentences, and titles should be capitalized. The names of countries, rivers, and states are all capitalized as well. Proper punctuation includes correct use of end marks, commas, semicolons, colons, and apostrophes. The conventions of written language also include making sure each sentence is complete. There should not be run-on or sentence fragments. Good penmanship is important, since it allows the reader to understand what has been written. The handwriting should be neat. Spelling is another important part of conventions. Words should be spelled correctly. To do this, it may be necessary to use a dictionary. By using these conventions, an author will be able to communicate more clearly.

Spelling

Words must be spelled correctly so that the reader can properly understand what the writer is saying. For example, in the sentence "We are going to go today to see a siens exhibit today about the moon," there is no way of understanding what the writer means by "siens." Is it silent? That does not make any sense. Is it signs? That does not make much sense either. Or is it science? That would make more sense. "We are going to see a science exhibit today about the moon." So it is very important to re-read what you write and check the spelling before turning in a final draft.

English I Practice Test #1

Practice Questions

Reading Test

Questions 1 – 12 pertain to the following passage:

Mammie

(1) Characters:
  ANTHONY – The young husband
  MANDIE – The young wife
  MAMMIE – Anthony's mother

(2) Setting:
Mammie's kitchen; the appliances are old, and a farmhouse table dominates the small room.

(3) The scene opens with Mandie clinging to Anthony. They are alone in the kitchen.

(4) MANDIE: Please don't leave me here with... her. She doesn't like me.

(5) ANTHONY: Of course she likes you. Don't be silly. Why wouldn't she like you?

(6) MANDIE: Oh, I don't know. She just doesn't. You don't know how she can be.

(7) ANTHONY: Don't I? I only lived with her for the first twenty years of my life.

(8) MANDIE: (pleading) Anthony, you can't go. Just take me with you. We can come back for dinner, just like you promised Mammie.

(9) ANTHONY: (taking Mandie firmly by the shoulders) No, Mandie. You're here, and you're staying. I'll only be gone for an hour or two. I promise to be back for dinner.

(10) MANDIE: But, Anthony—

(11) ANTHONY: Shush! She'll hear you—Mammie!

(12) Mammie enters, straightening her apron. She looks Mandie up and down. Anthony moves to kiss Mammie's cheek and Mandie reluctantly does the same.

(13) MAMMIE: Hello, Anthony. Hello, Amanda.

(14) ANTHONY: Well, Mammie, I'm afraid it's hello and goodbye for me. I'm off to my meeting. (He kisses Mandie.) You two girls have fun. I'll be back for dinner.

(15) Anthony exits. Mandie and Mammie look at each other for several seconds. The silence becomes uncomfortable. Finally, Mammie turns her back on Mandie and begins preparing dinner. She takes pots, pans, and ingredients out of the cupboards.

[handwritten margin note: They weren't talking but Mammie starts to cook.]

(16) MANDIE: (clearing her throat) So, um, what are you making for dinner?

(17) MAMMIE: (without turning around) Baked chicken. Rice. Asparagus.

(18) MANDIE: Oh. (Pauses) Could I help with something?

(19) Mammie wordlessly takes out a large pot and a bag of rice. She hands the items to Mandie and turns back to her work.

(20) MAMMIE: You can make the rice.

- 27 -

(21) Mandie stands very still, holding the rice and the pot. She bites her lip. She looks very frightened. Finally, Mammie turns around to face Mandie.

(22) MAMMIE: Well, child? What is it?

(23) MANDIE: (looking at the floor) I-I don't know how to make rice.

(24) MAMMIE: Don't know how to make rice? Don't be silly. Everyone knows how to make rice.

(25) MANDIE: (starting to cry) Everyone... except... me!

(26) Mammie sighs and wipes her hands on her apron. She comes over and takes the pot and the rice away from Mandie. She sets them on the table and gently chucks Mandie under the chin.

(27) MAMMIE: Come, child. It's nothing to cry over. Hush now. What can you cook?

(28) MANDIE: (sniffling) I can make brownies, I guess.

(29) MAMMIE: Good. (Patting Mandie awkwardly on the shoulder) Get to work, then.

(30) Mandie starts opening cupboard doors and pulling out ingredients. Mammie hands her a mixing bowl and measuring cups.

(31) MANDIE: Thank you.

(32) They work in silence for a while. After Mammie puts the chicken in the oven and puts the rice on to cook, she turns and watches Mandie work. Her face softens.

(33) MAMMIE: I suppose it's just as well, you know. Anthony always did like brownies better than rice. (She smiles and sits at the table.) I remember that when he was little, he always used to stick his finger into the middle brownie as soon as I took the pan from the oven. He always burned himself something terrible, but he couldn't let anyone else have that soft, gooey center brownie.

(34) MANDIE: (giggling) He still does that.

(35) MAMMIE: (shocked) No! A big, grown man like Anthony?

(36) MANDIE: Every time I make a batch of brownies.

(37) Mandie pours the batter into a brownie pan. Mammie watches her intently.

(38) MAMMIE: (motioning to the chair beside her) Come, child. Have a seat. Tell me more about my Anthony.

(39) Mandie sits and they chat for a while. Anthony reenters and looks surprised to see them sitting together.

(40) ANTHONY: (kissing Mandie) Hello, ladies. Something smells good. (He looks around.) And is that a pan of brownies waiting to go into the oven?

(41) MANDIE: Yes, Anthony. Now, go make yourself comfortable in the living room. We'll call you for dinner.

(42) ANTHONY: (bewildered) Well, okay... I guess. Are you sure you don't want me to stay in here?

(43) MANDIE: I'm sure. We have work to do. Now, go on.

(44) Anthony leaves, shaking his head and muttering to himself.

(45) MAMMIE: Besides, we can't talk about him when he's here!

(46) They both laugh and move to finish the dinner preparations, chatting amiably.

1. Which of the following is the best definition of the word "dominates" as it is used in paragraph 2?

    Ⓐ Diminishes

    🅑 Takes over

    Ⓒ Destroys

    Ⓓ Bosses around

2. How would you describe Mandie's feelings at the beginning of the play in relation to being left alone with Mammie?

    🅐 Desperate

    Ⓑ Excited

    Ⓒ Depressed

    Ⓓ Contented

3. Which paragraph best depicts Anthony's dismissive attitude toward Mandie's concerns?

    Ⓐ Paragraph 2

    Ⓑ Paragraph 3

    🅒 Paragraph 5

    Ⓓ Paragraph 7

4. Based on the information presented in the play, who is Mammie to Anthony?

    Ⓐ His aunt

    Ⓑ His grandmother

    Ⓒ His cousin

    🅓 His mother

5. How does the use of action and silence in this play contribute to the development of Mammie's character?

    Ⓐ It does not contribute to the development of Mammie's character

    Ⓑ It shows she is a poor communicator

    🅒 It demonstrates the awkwardness of her relationship with Mandie

    Ⓓ It shows her love for Anthony

6. Which paragraph best demonstrates Mammie's critical tendencies?

Ⓐ Paragraph 17

Ⓑ Paragraph 20

Ⓒ Paragraph 22

Ⓓ Paragraph 24

7. Which paragraph best indicates Mandie's feelings about Mammie?

Ⓐ Paragraph 3

Ⓑ Paragraph 4

Ⓒ Paragraph 8

Ⓓ Paragraph 10

8. What experience do Mandie and Mammie have in common that opens the door for them to bond with each other?

Ⓐ Anthony hates both of their cooking

Ⓑ Their rice always ends up overdone

Ⓒ Anthony sticks his finger into both their brownie batches

Ⓓ They both know how to bake brownies

9. What is the author's main purpose in writing this play?

Ⓐ To show that shared experiences provide relational connections

Ⓑ To emphasize the importance of getting along as a family

Ⓒ To highlight the detriments of familial disharmony

Ⓓ To exhibit a "slice of life" view of everyday Americana

10. Which of the following is a minor detail in this play?

Ⓐ Mammie is Mandie's mother-in-law

Ⓑ Mandie is afraid of Mammie

Ⓒ Anthony is leaving Mandie alone with Mammie for a while

Ⓓ The kitchen is small and cramped

11. Which of the following is an opinion, rather than a summary of this play?

Ⓐ This play examines the dynamics between a young wife and her mother-in-law

Ⓑ This play is a powerful, poignant look at the importance of communication

Ⓒ This play shows how common experiences can help build relationships

Ⓓ This play offers a look at the relationships of a man, his mother, and his wife

12. Which word in paragraph 43 best illustrates the newfound camaraderie between Mandie and Mammie?

Ⓐ We

Ⓑ Sure

Ⓒ Go

Ⓓ Work

Short Answer Question #1:

How does the relationship between Mandie and Mammie change over the course of this encounter? Support your answer with evidence from the text.

Questions 13 – 24 pertain to the following passage:
Vegetarian Victory

(1) I remember the day I came home and told my mom I was planning on becoming a vegetarian. It was the summer before my junior year of high school, and Mom just nodded and smiled knowingly. She assumed it was another phase, like my short-lived hot pink mohawk, or the now-passé pegged jeans. But it wasn't a phase. For the past decade, I have lived a vegetarian lifestyle because it is healthy, wallet-friendly, and environmentally wise.

(2) Most people are familiar with at least some of the health benefits of a vegetarian lifestyle. But many people also believe that sacrificing meat means sacrificing taste. Not true. I can easily get my required 50 grams of protein each day through beans, nuts, and seeds in dishes that are bursting with beautiful tastes. I use herbs and spices to make my food fun and flavorful. Best of all, by using plants to provide protein and punch in my diet I forego much of the fat and cholesterol that is so prevalent in animal products.

(3) By foregoing that fat and cholesterol, I also protect myself from a variety of common diseases and health conditions. Studies have shown, for example, that a vegetarian lifestyle reduces the risk of a variety of cancers and can even lower the incidence of Alzheimer's disease. In addition, a vegetarian

[Handwritten note in margin: "This guy chooses a to be a vegetarian but his mother thinks it's a phase."]

- 31 -

lifestyle has been shown to improve digestion, lower blood pressure and cholesterol levels, and protect against type II diabetes. In essence, I consider vegetables my super-weapon in the war against weariness!

(4) While the vegetarian lifestyle is clearly beneficial to my health, it also boosts my finances. Many people believe vegetarian foods—including fresh fruits and vegetables and alternative protein sources like soy—are just too expensive. To a certain extent, that may be true. But while the foods I eat may cost more than processed, packaged junk, my reward is fewer trips to the doctor and dentist. With the reduced incidence of disease comes a reduced need for treatments and medications. In the long run, the savings on medical costs more than makes up for the price of healthy food.

(5) The cost savings do not end with medical costs, however. I also save the money I used to spend on fast food and vending machines. My first two years of high school, I was a junk-food junkie. If you could get it at the drive-through or from a machine, I ate it. But after a while, all that junk made a sizeable dent in my wallet. When I became a vegetarian, I noticed that my cravings began to change. It didn't happen overnight, but over time I no longer craved the oily, greasy, and fatty food that drained my energy and my savings account. In fact, those types of foods actually started to make me sick. Now, I walk with a granola bar or tin of almonds in my pocket for convenient snacking. I'm saving my money and my health, all at once.

(6) Not only does my vegetarian lifestyle save my money and my health, it also helps save the environment. By choosing plant proteins over animal products, I am saving the lives of countless animals in my lifetime. I don't have to lie awake at night wondering about slaughterhouse horrors or inhumane living conditions. Whether or not all the stories of such things are true, I don't obsess about contributing to that industry anymore. More animals, raised more naturally, create a better prospect and future for our world.

(7) Many people do not realize that the livestock industry—run primarily for food consumption—is one of the largest contributors of greenhouse gases in our environment. Thousands of cattle milling about in dusty feed lots, long treks from farm to marketplace in large trucks, and other factors add up to a huge environmental impact. By choosing a vegetarian lifestyle, I reduce the demand for this industry, thereby reducing their level of production and both their carbon footprint and mine. My personal choice might not change the world, but I can do my best to change my corner of the community.

(8) Becoming a vegetarian is a very personal choice. I chose this lifestyle because it benefits my overall health and protects me from certain disease processes. I also chose this lifestyle because it benefits my finances by reducing my expenditures for health care and junk food. Finally, I chose this lifestyle because it benefits the environment, reducing the demands on the livestock industry and shrinking my carbon footprint. I know this choice works for me, but I never pressure my friends to become vegetarians. I tell them my story with pride, but I understand they must make the choice for themselves, and vegetarianism is not for everyone. Still, I never know when I might inspire someone else to have a vegetarian victory—just like mine!

13. Which of the following words is the best synonym for "passé" as it is used in paragraph 1?

Ⓐ Outdated

Ⓑ Fashionable

Ⓒ Foolish

Ⓓ Memorable

14. What are the three key benefits of a vegetarian lifestyle listed in this article?

Ⓐ Health benefits, social benefits, environmental benefits

Ⓑ Social benefits, financial benefits, environmental benefits

Ⓒ Health benefits, financial benefits, social benefits

Ⓓ Health benefits, financial benefits, environmental benefits

15. How long does the article say the author has been living a vegetarian lifestyle?

Ⓐ 5 years

Ⓑ 10 years

Ⓒ 15 years

Ⓓ The article does not give this information

16. What does the author compare the vegetarian lifestyle to in paragraph 3?

Ⓐ A cancer

Ⓑ A war

Ⓒ A disease

Ⓓ A weapon

17. What point of view was used to write this article?

Ⓐ First person

Ⓑ Second person

Ⓒ Third person

Ⓓ All of the above

18. Which of the following best describes the author's perspective in this article?

Ⓐ The vegetarian lifestyle is the only way to go

Ⓑ The vegetarian lifestyle doesn't work for most people

Ⓒ The vegetarian lifestyle offers many benefits

Ⓓ The vegetarian lifestyle is best lived short-term

19. According to the article, how many grams of protein does the author need each day?

Ⓐ 35

Ⓑ 45

Ⓒ 50

Ⓓ 10

20. What does paragraph 1 mean when it says, "Mom just nodded and smiled knowingly"?

Ⓐ Mom was, by nature, a very wise, happy person

Ⓑ Mom thought vegetarianism was just another phase

Ⓒ Mom was a vegetarian and was happy her child was too

Ⓓ Mom wasn't really listening because she was distracted

21. Which of the following is a controlling idea in this article?

Ⓐ Beans, nuts, and seeds can provide protein

Ⓑ The vegetarian lifestyle can improve finances

Ⓒ The vegetarian lifestyle can reduce cholesterol

Ⓓ Some slaughterhouses have inhumane conditions

22. Which of the following is an opinion about this article, rather than a summary?

Ⓐ This article clearly outlines the benefits of a vegetarian lifestyle

Ⓑ This article contains a lot of information about vegetarianism

Ⓒ This article uses opinions to guilt people into vegetarianism

Ⓓ This article urges people to consider a vegetarian lifestyle

23. Which of the following represents the author's main objective in writing this article?

(A) To open readers' eyes to the benefits of vegetarianism

(B) To force people to adopt a vegetarian lifestyle

(C) To clearly demonstrate the evils of eating animal products

(D) To illustrate the environmental impact of the livestock industry

24. Which paragraph best encapsulates the main ideas and purpose of this entire article?

(A) Paragraph 1

(B) Paragraph 3

(C) Paragraph 7

(D) Paragraph 8

Questions 25 – 29 pertain to the following short story:

Puck

(1) It was the second week of an unseasonably cool July. The sun had finally made a rare weekend appearance, and the suburban neighborhood sizzled with possibility. As the day slipped lazily into evening, sun-baked residents trickled back to their homes from the lakeshore and the park and the community pool. The air smelled of sunscreen, charcoal smoke, sweat, overcooked meat.

[handwritten: It was summer and it was good weather.]

(2) Will Jensen tossed a football across the yard to his best friend, Troy Coons. Dusk was settling around them, but the thought of retreating to the confines of the house seemed sacrilegious.

(3) "Can you believe we're going to college in a few weeks?" Troy asked, lobbing the ball back to Will.

(4) "What I can't believe is that you and I will be six hundred miles apart," Will said, catching the ball easily. "I don't think we've gone more than three days without seeing each other since kindergarten."

(5) "Except for when you had chicken pox," Troy said. "And the time I went to Hawaii with my grandparents. Remember how we begged them to let you come in my luggage?"

(6) Will laughed and tossed the ball back. "Those things don't count," he argued.

(7) The ball went sideways and Troy lunged for it, tripping over a ragged little terrier lounging lazily on the lawn. Troy collapsed in a tangled heap and the ball bounced down, just beyond his outstretched hand.

(8) "Puck!" Troy groaned. "No dogs on the field!"

(9) Will sauntered over and scooped up the little dog. He plopped down onto the crisp brown grass and laughed at Troy. Will reached over and rolled the ball toward Troy.

- 35 -

(10) "Don't blame Puck for your clumsiness," Will said, idly scratching the dog's fuzzy scalp. "How was he supposed to know you'd come stumbling through his daydreams?"

(11) Troy chuckled. Then they sat in silence as darkness swirled around them. Light glowed from windows thrown hopefully open to the faint breeze. Above them, the stars winked on in the charcoal sky. In the distance, leftover fireworks crackled and fizzed. The night was ripe with memories to be made.

(12) "Are you taking Puck with you?" Troy finally asked, breaking the silence.

(13) "Nah. No dogs in the dorm. Besides, Puck would hate being locked up in a room. He's spent the last sixteen years being king of the castle. He'll be happier here. That way he can greet me whenever I make it back home."

(14) Will lifted Puck and held him in mid-air. Puck wriggled playfully and licked Will's nose with his doughy pink tongue. Will laughed and set him down.

(15) "I sure will miss him, though," Will said, wiping Puck's saliva from his nose. "Puck's been a part of every memory I've had since I was really little."

(16) Troy faked a sniffle. "Stop, man. Just stop. I'm tearing up over here."

(17) Will punched Troy's arm good-naturedly. "Shut up!"

(18) A low, loud car careened around the corner, shattering the stupor of the summer night. Puck ran barking toward the car as it wove across the street like a wayward pinball.

(19) Seized with sudden panic, Will scrambled to his feet. "Puck, no! Come back!"

(20) As Will reached the sidewalk, Puck darted into the street. In a terrible, slow-motion montage, Will heard the tires squeal and Puck's bark turn to a startled yelp. Then the car sped away, and silence smothered the chaos.

(21) Will ran into the street. People peeked from doorways and windows, searching for the source of the commotion. Will fell beside Puck's limp body. Puck whimpered quietly and struggled to lick Will's hand. Then he was still.

(22) "No, Puck! No!" Will screamed. Shock rang in his ears and he was dizzy with emotion. Troy put a hand on Will's shoulder, but Will shook it off. He didn't want to be comforted. He wanted to wallow and writhe in the pool of pain that was slowly spreading through his soul.

(23) Every memory he had with Puck flooded his mind. This was not how it was supposed to be. Puck was supposed to be waiting for him when he came home from college. He was supposed to watch at the window as Will drove away and be there wagging with excitement whenever Will came home. He was supposed to be the constant in Will's changing life. This was not part of the plan.

(24) Will stayed in the road for a long time, crouched over Puck's familiar, lifeless body. He felt numb, empty, and emotionless. Finally, Will's mother led him gently from the street. Troy and Will's father gathered Puck's body carefully into a sheet. Neighbors watched in sympathy as the sorrowful party crossed the lawn.

(25) They walked in silence as darkness swirled around them. Lights still glowed from windows thrown hopefully open to the faint breeze. Above them, stars still winked on in the charcoal sky. In the distance, leftover fireworks still crackled and fizzed. Everything was the same, and nothing

was the same. Puck was gone. And Will knew things would never really be the same again.

25. In paragraph 2, what does "sacrilegious" mean?

Ⓐ Absurdly inappropriate

Ⓑ Nasty and evil

Ⓒ A waste of time

Ⓓ Holy and good

26. Which of the following best describes Will's attitude in paragraph 15?

Ⓐ Angry

Ⓑ Cheerful

Ⓒ Sentimental

Ⓓ Annoyed

27. What type of figurative language is used to describe the stars in paragraph 11?

Ⓐ Simile

Ⓑ Personification

Ⓒ Metaphor

Ⓓ Paradox

28. How is Puck's death an example of irony?

Ⓐ Will was worried about missing Puck while Will was away at college, and now he will miss him forever

Ⓑ Will wanted Puck to die so Will didn't have to think about him while he was away at college

Ⓒ Puck was always quiet and docile, but he was strangely driven to run after that one car

Ⓓ Troy hated Puck, and he wanted Puck to be hit by the passing car

29. Which of the following is a main idea in this story?

Ⓐ The passing car is playing loud music

Ⓑ Troy misses the ball when he trips over Puck

Ⓒ Will and Troy like to play football

Ⓓ Will has had Puck for a very long time

- 37 -

Questions 30 – 34 pertain to the following short story:
What I Will Always Remember

(1) I will always remember my grandfather, wiry and strong, hoisting me onto his shoulders as he showed me around the rail yard where he worked. His shock of shiny black hair glistened in the sunlight, flanked by silvery sideburns. High atop his shoulder, I owned the world. Everyone looked up to me, but I looked up to him. We played together like wayward children. He was larger than life, and I was proud he was my grandfather.

(2) I will always remember my grandfather, tainted with the first pangs of age, standing and proudly applauding at my high school graduation. He was grayer and weaker, but still robust. We stood eye to eye, but I still looked up to him. I craved his wisdom, his patience, his guidance. We talked together like two best pals. He was still larger than life, and I was proud he was my grandfather.

(3) I will always remember my grandfather, wrapped in the first throes of Parkinson's disease, watching me receive my college degree. He was paler and thinner and too weak to stand, but he applauded boisterously when my name was called. I towered above his wheelchair, but I still looked up to him. I needed his support, his affirmation, his companionship. We sat together like two old friends. He was still larger than life, and I was proud he was my grandfather.

(4) I will always remember my grandfather, lost in the last weeks of his life, sitting quietly with me on the front porch. His skin was translucent with the pallor of death, and his body was wracked by endless tremors. I fed him with a syringe, gently coaxing the food down his throat. He was shrunken and powerless, but I still looked up to him. We clung to our memories together like two sailors lost at sea. He was still larger than life, and I was proud he was my grandfather.

(5) Today I remembered my grandfather, cocooned in his flag-draped coffin as they lowered him into the ground. He was surrounded by those he had impacted in life. Today we honored a soldier, a worker, a teacher, a friend. We honored a husband, a father, a mentor, a guide. He was strong, even in weakness. He was wise, even in silence. He gave me everything, even when he had nothing to give, and I looked up to him. He will always be larger than life to me, and I will always be proud he was my grandfather.

30. In paragraph 4, what does "pallor" mean?

Ⓐ Brightness

🅑 Paleness

Ⓒ Jaundice

Ⓓ Darkness

31. How would you properly classify this piece of writing?

Ⓐ Informational essay

Ⓑ Fiction

Ⓒ Persuasive essay

Ⓓ Memoir

32. What is the author's main purpose in writing this piece?

Ⓐ To honor and say goodbye to Grandfather

Ⓑ To illustrate the ravages of age

Ⓒ To show the effects of Parkinson's disease

Ⓓ To chronicle Grandfather's life

33. What technique is used throughout this piece to increase its power and impact?

Ⓐ Plotting

Ⓑ Dialogue

Ⓒ Repetition

Ⓓ Citation

34. In paragraph 4, what image best illustrates Grandfather's powerlessness?

Ⓐ Sitting quietly on the porch

Ⓑ Being wracked with tremors

Ⓒ Being fed with a syringe

Ⓓ Having translucent skin

Questions 35 – 38 pertain to both short stories "Puck" and "What I Will Always Remember":

35. What theme do these two passages have most in common?

Ⓐ Loss of a loved one

Ⓑ The silence of summer

Ⓒ Companionship

Ⓓ Grandparents and friends

- 39 -

36. What is the difference in point of view between these two stories?

Ⓐ There is no difference in point of view between these two stories

Ⓑ One is written in third person and the other is written in first person

Ⓒ One is written in second person and the other is written in third person

Ⓓ One is written in first person and the other is written in second person

37. Why does the expression of grief seem more vivid in "Puck" than it does in "What I Will Always Remember"?

Ⓐ It does not seem more vivid in "Puck"

Ⓑ Will seems younger than the narrator in the other piece

Ⓒ The grief in "Puck" is more sudden and described in greater detail

Ⓓ Losing an animal is more painful than losing a grandparent

38. What is the primary similarity between paragraph 23 of "Puck" and paragraph 5 of "What I Will Always Remember"?

Ⓐ They both have seven sentences

Ⓑ They both express reminiscence in the face of loss

Ⓒ They are both centered on excessive emotion

Ⓓ They are both near the end of the piece

Short Answer Question #2:

How are the feelings of grief and loss similar in these two stories? How are they different? Support you answer with examples from both texts.

In both stories the main character lost a loved one. In Puck Troy wanted ~ Puck was supposed to be waiting for him when he comes home from college. In What I will always remember

Writing Test

Composition Prompt #1 – Literary Composition

Imagine you are stranded in an airport in an unfamiliar foreign country. What country are you in? What do you see? What do you hear? Who do you meet? Write a literary composition telling about your experience in detail.

Composition Prompt #2 – Expository Composition

Discuss the role of achievement in motivation for success. Do achievements motivate people to further success in the future? Or do achievements cause people to rest on their laurels? Explain your answer thoroughly.

Questions 39 – 48 pertain to the following short story:

The Saga of "Sparky"

(1) Sparky was a loser, but he didn't stay that way. (2) You probably know Sparky better by his given name: Charles Schulz. (3) Nicknamed Sparky when he was a child, Charles schulz endured years of struggle before he finally found success. (4) Eventually, the loser became a winner. (5) Thanks to the hard work and perseverance of Sparky, the world will always remember a boy named Charlie Brown and the rest of the Peanuts gang.

(6) Sparky was born Charles Monroe Schulz on November 26, 1922, and he grew up in Minneapolis, Minnesota, where he struggled to fit in socially. (7) He skipped two grades, and as a result he struggled with his studies. (8) He was also painfully shy, so he never dated. (9) In addition, Sparky was inert at most sports. (10) But he loved to draw, drawing was his dream.

(11) Sparky poured his heart and soul into his drawings during his high school years. (12) He had a particular love for cartooning, and he unsuccessfully submitted several cartoons to his yearbook. (13) In the late 1940s, when Sparky was in his mid-twenties, his dream began to come true. (14) Although he was devastated when the cartoons were rejected by the yearbook committee, he remained determined to make a living through his art someday. (15) He sold some cartoons to magazines and newspapers. (16) Someone finally appriciated his artistic ability.

(17) In 1950, Sparky created what would become his legacy; a comic called Peanuts. (18) The central character—Charlie Brown—was based on Sparky himself, and his lifelong struggle to fit in with the world around him. (19) Peanuts became an instant hit. (20) Adults and children alike were drawn to it because they could relate to the struggles of the characters.

(21) From its humble beginnings in the 1950s, Peanuts went on to become one of the most successful comics of all time. (22) Sparky lovingly hand-

- 41 -

drew each of the 18,000 Peanuts comic strips, and they eventually appointed in over 2000 newspapers in more than 75 countries. (23) The Peanuts characters have appeared in comic strips, television specials, coloring books, children's books, and a variety of other media. (24) Although Sparky died in 2000, his work lives on. (25) His comics are still seen in dozens of newspapers each week. (26) Through hard work, perseverance, and believing in himself, Sparky turned his loser's lot into a story of success.

39. Which of the following is the most appropriate correction for sentence 3?

Ⓐ Change Sparky to sparky

Ⓑ Change Nicknamed to Nick-named

Ⓒ Remove the comma after child

Ⓓ Change Charles schulz to Charles Schulz

40. Which sentence in paragraph 1 functions as the thesis statement for this composition?

Ⓐ Sentence 2

Ⓑ Sentence 5

Ⓒ Sentence 3

Ⓓ Sentence 1

41. In sentence 9, what change is necessary?

Ⓐ Change inert to inept

Ⓑ Remove the comma after addition

Ⓒ Change Sparky to sparky

Ⓓ Change most to many

42. What change, if any, should be made in sentence 10?

Ⓐ No change is necessary

Ⓑ Remove the comma

Ⓒ Replace the comma with a semicolon

Ⓓ Replace the comma with a colon

43. What change would most improve the organization of the third paragraph of this composition?

    Ⓐ Swap sentences 13 and 14

    Ⓑ Move sentence 13 to the beginning of the paragraph

    Ⓒ Swap sentences 11 and 16

    Ⓓ Move sentence 12 to the end of the paragraph

44. What change, if any, should be made in sentence 16?

    Ⓐ No change is necessary

    Ⓑ Change finally to finaly

    Ⓒ Change appriciated to appreciated

    Ⓓ Change artistic to autistic

45. What change, if any, is needed in sentence 17?

    Ⓐ No change is necessary

    Ⓑ Replace the semicolon with a colon

    Ⓒ Replace the semicolon with a period

    Ⓓ Remove the semicolon

46. What punctuation change, if any, should be made in sentence 18?

    Ⓐ No change is necessary

    Ⓑ Remove the dashes

    Ⓒ Replace the second dash with a comma

    Ⓓ Replace the first dash with a colon

47. How does sentence 21 function as a transition between paragraph 4 and paragraph 5?

    Ⓐ Sentence 21 does not function as a transition

    Ⓑ It talks about a topic previously mentioned

    Ⓒ It demonstrates transition with the phrase "went on"

    Ⓓ It connects the history of Peanuts with the success of Sparky

- 43 -

48. In sentence 22, what word would be most appropriate to replace the misused word "appointed"?

Ⓐ Approximated

🅱 Appeared

Ⓒ Appropriated

Ⓓ Appositioned

Questions 49 – 58 pertain to the following essay:

The Very Best Season

(1) Ice cream cones shrink and drip in the stiffling heat. (2) Cool pools shimmer like a welcoming oasis. (3) The blazing sun hangs lazily for hours in the breathtakingly blue sky. (4) It's summer, and the whole world seems more content. (5) Summer is the very best season for three main reasons.

(6) First, Summer is the best season because school is out and the days are long and lazy. (7) Without structure and schedule, the nights were late and the afternoons roll on forever. (8) There is no homework, no pressure, and no deadlines. (9) There is no blaring alarm clock, just the endless cadence of birds and sprinklers and kids playing in the streets. (10) Everything feels more simpler and more relaxed.

(11) That sense of relaxation brings the second reason summer is the best season: the pace of life is slower. (12) No one seems to be in a hurry. (13) It is the season of hamocks and vacations and sandy seashores. (14) It is a time when the whole hectic, hurried world seems to pause and take a deep, cleansing breath. (15) The endless days and hazy nights seem to add to the pleasant stupor. (16) All is calm, and all is bright.

(17) Despite the universal sense of relaxation summer is also the best season because there is so much to do. (18) Warm, dry weather lends itself perfectly to outdoor activities: camping in the cool, quiet woods; swimming in a crystal-clear stream; sunning on an emerald carpet of fragrant grass. (19) It is also the season of fairs, festivals, and farmers' markets. (20) There is never a shortage of fun.

(21) While every season of the year has its own unique charms, summer will always be the best season to me. (22) The long, lazy, school-free days are loved by me. (23) I love the slower, more relaxed pace of life. (24) Finally, I love the many fun activities that can fill the empty hours. (25) All of these things—and many more—make summer the very best season.

49. What change, if any, needs to be made in sentence 1?

Ⓐ No change is necessary

Ⓑ Change stiffling to stifling

Ⓒ Change cream to Cream

Ⓓ Insert a comma after shrink

50. Which sentence functions as the thesis statement for this essay?

Ⓐ Sentence 1

Ⓑ Sentence 4

Ⓒ Sentence 5

Ⓓ Sentence 10

51. In sentence 6, what correction, if any, is necessary?

Ⓐ No correction is necessary

Ⓑ Remove the comma after first

Ⓒ Insert a comma after season

Ⓓ Change Summer to summer

52. Which of the following is the best version of sentence 7?

Ⓐ Without structure and schedule, the nights are late and the afternoons roll on forever

Ⓑ Without structure and schedule, the nights are late and the afternoons rolled on forever

Ⓒ Without structure and schedule, the nights were late and the afternoons rolled on forever

Ⓓ The sentence is correct as it is written.

53. What correction, if any, is needed in sentence 10?

Ⓐ No correction is needed.

Ⓑ Change more simpler to simpler

Ⓒ Change feels to felt

Ⓓ Insert a comma after simpler

54. What change, if any, is needed in sentence 11?

   Ⓐ No change is needed

   Ⓑ Replace the colon with a semicolon

   Ⓒ Replace the colon with a comma

   Ⓓ Remove the colon

55. In sentence 13, what spelling error needs to be corrected?

   Ⓐ Change season to session

   Ⓑ Change hamocks to hammocks

   Ⓒ Change seashores to seeshores

   Ⓓ There is no spelling error in sentence 13

56. What change, if any, should be made in sentence 17?

   Ⓐ No change is necessary.

   Ⓑ Insert a comma after season

   Ⓒ Insert a comma after Despite

   Ⓓ Insert a comma after relaxation

57. What is the error in sentence 22?

   Ⓐ It is a sentence fragment

   Ⓑ It is a run-on sentence

   Ⓒ It has passive construction

   Ⓓ It has parallel structure

58. What correction, if any, needs to be made in sentence 25?

   Ⓐ No correction is necessary

   Ⓑ Remove the dashes

   Ⓒ Replace the first dash with a colon

   Ⓓ Replace the second dash with a comma

Questions 59 – 68 pertain to the following short story:

Volunteer Fisherman

(1) As a new volunteer at the youth center, I was expected to help out with activities, like the upcoming fishing field trip. (2) When the director asked me to come along, I excepted right away. (3) I had never been fishing, but it looked easy enough on TV. (4) You just tossed a line into the water and waited for a fish to bite. (5) How hard could that be? (6) It ended up being much harder than I expected.

(7) Upon arrival at the Turner Family Trout Farm, I was assigned three rambunctious Kindergartners as my charges for the day. (8) They were tense with excited energy and frequently ran off in various directions. (9) Keeping them together while herding them toward the equipment shed took every ounce of my focus and every shred of my patience. (10) Finally, we found ourselves in line for poles and bait.

(11) Once we had collected our poles and bait, we marched our way to an empty spot on the rocky banks of a green-black pond. (12) I ordered the boys to line up so that I could bait their hooks. (13) When the first one thrust his read plastic cup full of soil and writhing nightcrawlers into my face, I almost gagged. (14) I looked away and plunged my fingers into the dirt, closing them on the first worm I could find. (15) I pulled him from the dirt and held him up triumphantly. (16) The boys clapped and cheered. (17) Success!

(18) I soon learned pulling the worm from the plastic cup was among the easiest parts of fishing. (19) The hook would not penetrate his tough skin. (20) Baiting the hook posed a whole new set of challenges. (21) The worm curled its slimy ridges eagerly around my dirty fingers. (22) I poked through my finger three times before I finally got the worm onto the hook. (23) I breathed a sigh of relief before I realized, I had two more hooks to bait.

(24) Finally, with all the hooks baited, I tried casting the first rod. (25) The hook plopped into the water about two feet out—not the 30-foot cast I had envisioned—and to my horror, the worm floated away. (26) I baited the hook again in discouraged disgust and finally got all the lines cast about five feet out. (27) My fishing wouldn't win any awards, but my kindergarden protégés were happy, and that was good enough for me.

(28) After nearly an hour of our fishing adventure had passed, we had three trout awkwardly dangling from our stringer. (29) The boys were thrilled, and I was exhausted. (30) Between baiting hooks, reeling in catches, and keeping the boys from falling into the pond, my energy was spent. (31) But when the whistle blew to load the bus for the trip home, I felt strangely saddened. (32) Despite the headaches and harrowing challenges, I was proud of all I had accomplished that day. (33) And I knew the next time they needed a volunteer fisherman, myself would be the first to sign up!

- 47 -

59. Which of the following is the most appropriate correction for sentence 2?

Ⓐ No correction is needed

Ⓑ Change along to alone

Ⓒ Change excepted to accepted

Ⓓ Change right to write

60. Which sentence functions as the thesis statement for this piece?

Ⓐ Sentence 1

Ⓑ Sentence 6

Ⓒ Sentence 7

Ⓓ Sentence 10

61. What is the proper correction for the capitalization error in sentence 7?

Ⓐ Change Farm to farm

Ⓑ Change Trout to trout

Ⓒ Change Kindergartners to kindergartners

Ⓓ There is no capitalization error in sentence 7

62. What correction, if any, needs to be made in sentence 13?

Ⓐ No correction is needed

Ⓑ Change writhing to rising

Ⓒ Change thrust to thirst

Ⓓ Change read to red

63. Where should sentence 19 be placed to improve the organization of this essay?

Ⓐ Before sentence 18

Ⓑ Right where it is

Ⓒ After sentence 20

Ⓓ After sentence 21

- 48 -

64. What change, if any, is necessary in sentence 22?

Ⓐ No change is necessary

Ⓑ Change through to threw

Ⓒ Change three to 3

Ⓓ Change onto to into

65. How can sentence 23 be corrected?

Ⓐ Sentence 23 is correct as it is written.

Ⓑ Remove the comma

Ⓒ Replace the comma with a semicolon

Ⓓ Replace the comma with a dash

66. What spelling correction, if any, is appropriate in sentence 27?

Ⓐ No spelling correction is needed

Ⓑ Change kindergarden to kindergarten

Ⓒ Change protégés to protoges

Ⓓ Change enough to enuogh

67. What change, if any, needs to be made in sentence 28?

Ⓐ No change is needed.

Ⓑ Change had passed to have passed

Ⓒ Change had three to have three

Ⓓ Change dangling to dangled

68. What type of error is present in sentence 33?

Ⓐ There is no error in sentence 33.

Ⓑ There is a comma splice

Ⓒ There is a verb form error

Ⓓ There is a misused reflexive pronoun

Answers and Explanations

TEKS Standard §110.31(b)(1)(A)
1. B: In Paragraph 2, "dominates" means "takes over." The author is using the word to show how much of the small room is taken up by the large table.

TEKS Standard §110.31(b)(5) and (4) and Figure: 19 TAC §110.30(b)(110.31)
2. A: "Desperate" is the best choice because to describe Mandie's feelings in the beginning of the play about being left alone with Mammie. She is clinging to her husband and begging him not to leave her alone with his mother.

TEKS Standard §110.31(b)(5) and (4) and Figure: 19 TAC §110.30(b)(110.31)
3. C: Paragraph 5 clearly shows Anthony's dismissive attitude when he calls Mandie "silly."

TEKS Standard §110.31(b)(5) and (4) and Figure: 19 TAC §110.30(b)(110.31)
4. D: The "Characters" section of this play (Paragraph 1) describes Mammie as Anthony's mother.

TEKS Standard §110.31(b)(5) and (4) and Figure: 19 TAC §110.30(b)(110.31)
5. C: Silence and action contribute to the development of Mammie's character by showing how awkwardly she relates to Mandie.

TEKS Standard §110.31(b)(5) and (4) and Figure: 19 TAC §110.30(b)(110.31)
6. D: Paragraph 24 clearly shows Mammie's critical tendencies in the way she responds to Mandie's ignorance, when she tells her to stop being silly, because everyone knows how to cook rice.

TEKS Standard §110.31(b)(5) and (4) and Figure: 19 TAC §110.30(b)(110.31)
7. B: Paragraph 4 shows Mandie's feelings about Mammie when she says, "She doesn't like me."

TEKS Standard §110.31(b)(5) and (4) and Figure: 19 TAC §110.30(b)(110.31)
8. C: Mandie's relationship with Mammie begins to improve when Mammie tells Mandy that when Anthony was growing up, he loved to stick his finger into the middle brownie after she baked them, and Mandy replies by laughing about the fact that he still does it.

TEKS Standard §110.31(b)(5) and (4) and Figure: 19 TAC §110.30(b)(110.31)
9. A: is The most important lesson of this short play is that people can get along with each other better when they share common interests or experiences.

TEKS Standard §110.31(b)(5) and (4) and Figure: 19 TAC §110.30(b)(110.31)
10. D: The fact that the kitchen is small and cramped doesn't have much of a bearing on the story at all, but the other three answer choices represent important points in the play.

TEKS Standard §110.31(b)(5) and (4) and (9)(A)

11. B is the correct answer because it is an expression of a person's view of the play, using the words "powerful" and "poignant," making it an opinion. A summary gives a factual description of a play, while an opinion is one person's unique take on it.

TEKS Standard §110.31(b)(5) and (4) and Figure: 19 TAC §110.30(b)(110.31)

12. A: When Mandie says "*we* have work to do", it illustrates the newfound camaraderie between herself and Mammie.

Sample Short Answer #1:

> In the beginning of this play, the relationship between Mammie and Mandie is clearly tense. This is best demonstrated in paragraph 4, when Mandie says, "She doesn't like me." It is also shown in the stage directions in paragraph 12, where the play states Mandie "reluctantly" kisses Mammie, and in paragraph 15, when Mammie "turns her back on Mandie."
>
> In contrast, their relationship at the end of the play shows a sense of camaraderie. They have bonded over the common link of Anthony. This is best shown in paragraph 38 when Mammie invites Mandie to have a seat with her and talk about Anthony. It is also shown in paragraph 43, when Mandie shoos Anthony from the kitchen and refers to herself and Mammie as "we."

TEKS Standard §110.31(b)(1)(A)

13. A: The word "passé" means "outdated."

TEKS Standard §110.31(b)(10) and Figure: 19 TAC §110.30(b)(110.31)

14. D: The three key benefits discussed in this article are health benefits, financial benefits, and environmental benefits.

TEKS Standard §110.31(b)(10) and Figure: 19 TAC §110.30(b)(110.31)

15. B: Paragraph 1 indicates that the author has been a vegetarian for a decade, which is 10 years.

TEKS Standard §110.31(b)(10) and Figure: 19 TAC §110.30(b)(110.31)

16. D: In paragraph 3, the vegetarian lifestyle is compared to a weapon.

TEKS Standard §110.31(b)(10) and Figure: 19 TAC §110.30(b)(110.31)

17. A: This article is written in first-person point of view.

TEKS Standard §110.31(b)(10)

18. C: The author's perspective is that being a vegetarian offers many benefits, but we know she doesn't feel that "it's the only way to go", because she says that she never pressures her friends to become vegetarians.

TEKS Standard §110.31(b)(10) and Figure: 19 TAC §110.30(b)(110.31)(B)

19. C: Paragraph 2 indicates that the author needs 50 grams of protein each day.

TEKS Standard §110.31(b)(10) and Figure: 19 TAC §110.30(b)(110.31)(B)

20. B: In Paragraph 1, when the author says, "Mom just nodded and smiled knowingly", she follows it up in the next sentence by stating that her mother was assuming that vegetarianism was just going to another of the author's many phases.

TEKS Standard §110.31(b)(10) and Figure: 19 TAC §110.30(b)(110.31)(B)

21. B: A controlling idea is an idea that represents one of the main points the author is making. One of her main points is that being a vegetarian improves one's finances. She makes the other points, too, but they are subordinate to her overall main points.

TEKS Standard §110.31(b)(10) and (9)(A)

22. C is the only answer choice that is a personal opinion of this article, rather than a fact-based description of it.

TEKS Standard §110.31(b)(10)

23. A best represents the author's main objective in this article, which is to show people the benefits of vegetarianism that they may not be aware of. She is certainly not trying to force anyone to become a vegetarian. She does discuss the ill effects of factory farms and eating meat on animals and the environment, but they are minor points, not her main one.

TEKS Standard §110.31(b)(10)

24. D: Paragraph 8 best encapsulates both the main ideas and purpose of the article. As it's the final paragraph in the piece, this should come as no surprise, because many authors of short articles such as this one will use their final paragraph to recap and summarize the whole.

TEKS Standard §110.31(b)(1)(A)

25. A: is the best choice because the best definition of "sacrilegious" as it appears in paragraph 2 is "absurdly inappropriate." This is not the literal meaning of "sacreligious", which means "not showing proper respect to something holy." The author is using the word figuratively, to say that going inside would be a complete waste of the nice weather, and completely out of place because of all the activity that had taken place outdoors that day.

TEKS Standard §110.31(b)(5) and Figure: 19 TAC §110.30(b)(110.31)

26. C: Will's attitude in Paragraph 15 is best described as sentimental, because he's expressing strong emotions.

TEKS Standard §110.31(b)(7)

27. B: Personification is used to describe the stars in Paragraph 11, when the author says the stars "winked." Winking is something that human beings do, and personification is attributing a human trait or actions to something that isn't human.

TEKS Standard §110.31(b)(7)(A)

28. A best illustrates how Puck's death is an example of irony, which is when something happens in a way that's the opposite of what one would expect.

TEKS Standard §110.31(b)(5) and Figure: 19 TAC §110.30(b)(110.31)

29. D is the only option that is a main idea in this story. The other three answer selections are all supporting ideas, not main ideas in the story.

30. B: "Pallor" means "paleness."

TEKS Standard §110.31(b)(6)
31. D: This essay is best classified as a memoir, or a personal recollection by a writer.

TEKS Standard §110.31(b)(6) and Figure: 19 TAC §110.30(b)(110.31)
32. A: The main purpose of this piece is to honor and say goodbye to Grandfather. The other answer choices represent aspects of the piece, but none of them are the main reason the author had in mind for writing this.

TEKS Standard §110.31(b)(6) and Figure: 19 TAC §110.30(b)(110.31)
33. C: The author uses repetition in this piece to increase its power and impact. Every paragraph but the last begins with the phrase "I will always remember my grandfather", which is followed by a snapshot of what he was like at that point in his life.

TEKS Standard §110.31(b)(6) and Figure: 19 TAC §110.30(b)(110.31)
34. C: Being fed with a syringe is the image that most strongly illustrates Grandfather's powerlessness, because being unable to feed one's self is a state of extreme weakness. The other answer choices represent age-related problems, but not powerlessness.

TEKS Standard §110.31(b)(2)(A) and Figure: 19 TAC §110.30(b)(110.31)
35. A: The common theme that most unites these passages is loss of a loved one. This is not to imply that the loss of a dog is equivalent to the loss of a grandparent, but only that both pieces are about deeply felt personal loss.

TEKS Standard Figure: 19 TAC §110.30(b)(110.31)
36. B: The first piece is written in third-person point of view and the second is in first-person point of view.

TEKS Standard Figure: 19 TAC §110.30(b)(110.31)
37. C: The reason the grief in "Puck" seems more vivid is because it comes as a sudden shock, whereas in the other piece, the grandfather's decline takes place over years, and is the natural process most people will experience as they age.

TEKS Standard Figure: 19 TAC §110.30(b)(110.31)
38. B: Both paragraphs express reminiscence in the face of loss.

Sample Short Answer #2:

We see grief and loss in the emotional pain of both stories. This is especially evident in paragraph 24 of "Puck" when Will stays crouched over Puck's lifeless body. In "What I Will Always Remember," it is shown in paragraph 4 when the narrator says, "We clung to our memories together like two sailors lost at sea." Both instances demonstrate a desire to hold onto the past in the face of a grief-filled future.

On the other hand, the narrator of "What I Will Always Remember" seems more pragmatic, prepared for, and disconnected from Grandfather's death.

In "Puck," Will's reaction to Puck's death is much more visceral, as evidenced by his screaming and the description of his physical grief reaction in paragraph 22.

Sample Composition #1 – Literary Composition:
Alone, But Not Lonely

My flight was delayed—again. The next plane wasn't scheduled to leave until morning. That meant I had to spend the night in the airport. Already the shopkeepers were dropping gates across their darkened shops. With every clanking gate, the airport emptied further. It was a far cry from the typical, 24-hour bustle of the busy airport at home.

Down some unseen hallway, a baby cried. A man's voice echoed sharply in a distant corridor. Subdued reggae music drifted faintly through the nearly-empty terminal from the only shop that remained open. It was a combination coffee shop and magazine stand, and a young man with thick dreadlocks lounged behind the counter, sipping a coffee and browsing through a magazine.

Across the terminal from where I sat, a scruffy-looking custodian pushed a wide broom over the waxy floor. He whistled a chaotic counterpoint to the reggae. Every so often, he burst into song for a few notes, and then returned to his whistling. I studied his tufted hair and grizzled beard. His clothes hung from his narrow body like a scarecrow, and he danced through his work with a smile.

As he neared the coffee shop/magazine stand, the custodian called out to the young man behind the counter. They chatted for a few moments and then motioned toward me, continuing to talk and laugh. I was suddenly vividly aware of the emptiness of the terminal. I was alone, a young girl far from home, and I was afraid. When the young man with dreadlocks started across the terminal toward me, I considered running, but I was frozen to my seat with fatigue and fear.

"You not from here, I see," he said, taking a seat beside me. His voice had the unmistakable island lilt, and his smile seemed warm. "Look here—you don' hafta sit here by youself. Come on in my shop."

"I don't have any money left," I admitted.

"No problem, mon," he said, standing and pulling me to my feet. He grabbed my carry-on and slung it over his shoulder. "I make you a coffee and we jus' talk. It will make di time go fasta."

It did make the time go faster. Damian—that was his name—and I talked for hours and became good friends. That night, in a strange, faraway place, Damian taught me about reaching out without fear. Most of all, he taught me that being alone didn't mean I had to be lonely. Friends are waiting for me wherever I choose to make them.

Sample Composition #2 – Expository Composition:

Achievements: Springboards to Success

I can still vividly remember the moment I won my first speech competition. With the announcement of my name and the thundering applause came a trickle of disbelief followed by a flood of personal pride. That achievement became the first of many, a springboard to a new hobby and a career path. Achievements are important motivators for future success because they build confidence, fuel desire, and encourage dreaming.

Achievements contribute to future success by building confidence. Before I won that speech competition, I thought I could never speak in front of people or present information in public. After the contest, I had a new belief in myself and my abilities. Life's constant barrage of small setbacks can sap our strength and our belief in ourselves. The simple knowledge that we can succeed at something fills us with an assurance that future success is possible. Each achievement serves as the foundation for the next, creating a positive pyramid of possibilities for the future.

In addition to building confidence, achievement fuels desire. After I won that speech competition, I wanted to win more. I wanted to succeed at the regional and national levels. I wanted to see how far I could go. When we achieve goals, we tend to desire bigger and better things. Each accomplishment in life fuels our desires and gives the hope and drive necessary to achieve future success. Achievements are like food for the soul, nourishing our desires and spurring us on to further greatness.

While achievements build confidence and fuel desires, they also encourage dreaming. From the success of the speech competition, I dreamed of speaking to large crowds, of a career as a teacher or speaker or professor. I dreamed that I could even be president, speaking my mind to the world. The confidence and desire established by achievement give wings to our hopes and free our minds to dream. Achievement gives us new ideas and expands our horizons. We can dream with abandon of all that is possible in the future and all we might someday accomplish. Dreaming is the first blueprint for life's grandest future castles of success.

Achievements are the springboards for success. I am proud of all I've done since that speech competition, developing my skills and doing things I never thought possible. It is all thanks to the power of achievements. They build our confidence, allowing us to believe in ourselves. They fuel our desires, allowing us to yearn for future accomplishment. Lastly, they encourage our dreaming, allowing us to envision the vast possibilities that the future holds. Achievements give us permission to be our best, opening doors to success and all that life can hold.

TEKS Standard §110.31(b)(18)(A)

39. D: Charles schulz should be changed to Charles Schulz.

TEKS Standard §110.31(b)(15)(A)(iii)

40. B: Sentence 5 functions as the thesis statement for this composition. It briefly tells the reader what he'll learn in the piece, in much more depth. It reveals the author's main points.

TEKS Standard §110.31(b)(13)(C)

41. A: Changing "inert" to "inept" corrects the meaning of sentence, because inert is not the correct word choice here. It means motionless, unable to move, barely moving, etc., while "inept" means unskilled. It's much more likely that the author meant to say that Charles Schulz was unskilled at sports, rather than saying that he just stood motionless while engaged in athletic endeavors.

TEKS Standard § 110.31(b)(13)(D) and (18)(B)

42. C: Sentence 10 is a comma splice with two independent clauses, which is incorrect. Two independent clauses should be joined by a semicolon, not a comma.

TEKS Standard §110.31(b)(13)

43. A: Swapping sentences 13 and 14 will improve the organization and flow of paragraph 3, because they are out of chronological order as written. This is jarring and confusing to the reader.

TEKS Standard §110.31(b)(13)(D) and (19)

44. C: The word "appreciated" is a misspelling; the correct spelling is "appreciated."

TEKS Standard §110.31(b)(13)(D) and (18)(B)

45. B: A colon is the correct punctuation in sentence 17, not a semicolon.

TEKS Standard §110.31(b)(18)(B)

46. A: Sentence 18 is correct as written.

TEKS Standard §110.31(b)(15)(A)(ii)

47. D: The author has been talking about Sparky's struggles to succeed, and the history of the Peanuts strip, and in the final paragraph he demonstrates just how successful Sparky became, all thanks to the popularity of Peanuts. Sentence 21 serves as a transitional sentence between these two aspects of the article.

TEKS Standard §110.31(b)(13)(C)

48. B: The word "appeared" is the correct word to replace the misused word "appointed."

TEKS Standard §110.31(b)(13)(D) and (19)

49. B: The word "stiffling" is a misspelling; it should be "stifling. "

TEKS Standard §110.31(b)(16)(A)

50. C: Sentence 5 functions as the thesis statement for this essay. It's a brief summation of what the author intends to demonstrate in the entire article. Demonstrating that summer is the best season by giving three reasons is the author's main purpose in writing this piece.

TEKS Standard §110.31(b)(18)(A)

51. D: In normal usage, the names of the seasons should not be capitalized, so "Summer" should be "summer."

TEKS Standard §110.31(b)(13)(D) and (17)(A)(i)

52. A is correct because both verbs are now in the present tense. As written, the first verb in the sentence, "were" is in past tense, while the second verb, "roll", is in present tense. This is unacceptable. The article is written using the present tense for every other verb, so both verbs in this sentence should also be in present tense.

TEKS Standard §110.31(b)(17)

53. B: The word "simpler" is the correct comparative form of "simple." The phrase "more simple" would also be acceptable here, in order to match the construction of "more relaxed", but "more simpler" is never acceptable.

TEKS Standard §110.31(b)(17)

54. A: No change is necessary; sentence 11 is correct as written.

TEKS Standard §110.31(b)(13)(D) and (19)

55. B: The word "hamocks" is a misspelling; it should be "hammocks."

TEKS Standard §110.31(b)(18)(B)(ii)

56. D: A comma should follow the word "relaxation" in order to separate the introductory phrase from the main clause of the sentence.

TEKS Standard §110.31(b)(17)(A)(i)

57. C: Sentence 22 is written with passive construction, which is very awkward sounding. It should be written in the active voice: "I love the long, lazy, school-free days."

TEKS Standard §110.31(b)(18)(B)

58. A: Sentence 25 is correct as written.

TEKS Standard §110.31(b)(13)(C)

59. C: The word "accepted" is the proper word to use in this sentence. The author has either badly misspelled it, or has misunderstood the meaning of "excepted", which means "not included."

TEKS Standard §110.31(b)(15)(A)(iii)

60. B: Sentence 6 functions as the thesis statement in the essay. When the author begins her adventure, she assumes it will be very easy, but by the end of her day, she has learned that helping out on a fishing field trip was much more difficult than she had anticipated. That is the main point, or thesis, of this short essay.

TEKS Standard §110.31(b)(18)(A)

61. C: The word "kindergartners" should not be capitalized.

TEKS Standard §110.31(b)(13)(C)

62. C: In sentence 13, changing "read" to "red" is correct. The word "read" is a verb meaning "having looked at and understood"; "red" is a color.

TEKS Standard §110.31(b)(13)

63. D: The proper position for sentence 19 is after sentence 21. As written, the sentences in this paragraph are not in proper order, which is confusing for readers.

TEKS Standard §110.31(b)(13) and (17)
64. A: Sentence 22 is correct as written.

TEKS Standard §110.31(b)(18)(B)
65. B: The comma in sentence 23 is unnecessary.

TEKS Standard §110.31(b)(13)(D) and (19)
66. B: The word "kindergarden" is a misspelling; it should be "kindergarten."

TEKS Standard §110.31(b)(13) and (17)
67. A: Sentence 28 is correct as it is written.

TEKS Standard §110.31(b)(17)(A)
68. D: The reflexive pronoun "myself" is misused in sentence 33. It should be replace with "I."

English I Practice Test #2

Practice Questions

Questions 1 -5 pertain to the following passage:

Caged

(1) I am caged.
(2) Dim, dark, dank,
(3) Depressing metal bars
(4) Are my home,
(5) My window on the world.
(6) But for one hour each day—
(7) Sixty precious, priceless minutes—
(8) I am led from the dungeon
(9) Into the bright, blinding light.
(10) That is my sanctuary,
(11) Wrapped in chain link
(12) And barbed wire.
(13) The air is sweeter,
(14) Tinged with freedom
(15) And fragranced with memories
(16) Of a lifetime so long ago
(17) It has almost been forgotten.
(18) I bathe in the welcome warmth,
(19) Cleanse my soul in the newborn breeze.
(20) I confess my sins
(21) In the brazen light of day,
(22) And hope springs eternal once again.
(23) But then they come.
(24) My time is up.
(25) Another hour of life has expired.
(26) And I return to the depths
(27) Of despair, discouragement, defeat.
(28) Freedom, forgiveness, and faith are forgotten.
(29) I am caged.

1. What is the connotation of the word "dungeon" in line 8?

Ⓐ The narrator lives in the basement of a castle

Ⓑ This poem is set in medieval times

Ⓒ The narrator's life is dark and unrelenting

Ⓓ The narrator is uncomfortable with life

- 59 -

2. What is the setting for this poem?

    Ⓐ A prison

    Ⓑ A farm

    Ⓒ A house

    Ⓓ A school

3. Which literary device is used throughout this poem to underscore the repetitive nature of the narrator's life?

    Ⓐ Simile

    Ⓑ Paradox

    Ⓒ Onomatopoeia

    Ⓓ Alliteration

4. What point of view is used in this poem?

    Ⓐ First person

    Ⓑ Second person

    Ⓒ Third person

    Ⓓ All of the above

5. What do lines 18-22 reference?

    Ⓐ The narrator's love of sunny days

    Ⓑ The narrator's desire for a fresh start

    Ⓒ The narrator's anger at the circumstances

    Ⓓ The narrator's memories of a normal life

Questions 6 – 10 pertain to the following short story:

Freedom Run

(1) The rattle of the key fumbling in the lock sent a shudder down her spine. He was home. Megan gulped down her emotions and fixed her face into a plastic smile. With a sigh, she clicked off the late show. The door swung open, and he stumbled inside.

(2) "There'sh my little Meggie-May," he crooned, slurring his words into one jumbled strand. "Howsh it goin'? What you up to tonight, little one?"

(3) He staggered toward her, arms outstretched. She stood, numb and motionless, like an observer in an overplayed scene. The same dialogue. The same motions. Rehearsed every night for some unscheduled performance. It was familiar. Too familiar.

- 60 -

(4) He tripped on a chair leg as he passed the dining table. The pleasant face instantly darkened as the shadow of impending rage fell. He swore loudly and turned on Megan.

(5) Why don't you clean up this pigsty," he yelled, the words clearer, colder, chilling.

(6) In two long strides, he crossed to where she still stood, rooted to the floor. She had learned long ago that backing away only prolonged the misery. His hand fell heavy across her cheek.

(7) "Lazy, good-for-nothing child," he screamed. He swore again, throwing her into the wall. "Ungrateful!"

(8) She no longer cringed as the blows landed. When he knocked her to the ground, she instinctively curled around herself, forming a tight little ball of misery. His feet crashed clumsily into her body, and she waited for it to end. In a while, it would be over. It never lasted forever.

(9) When the blows stopped, Megan struggled to her feet. She could taste the tang of blood on her split lip. She could feel the swelling in her eye. She watched him watching her. Then his face crumpled into a broken sob. He pulled her to his chest and stroked her hair.

(10) "I'm so sorry, Meggie-May. I don't mean to hurt you, darling." He sobbed louder. "Please forgive me, my little Meggie-May. I just get so mad sometimes. I won't do it again. Promise."

(11) Megan held him awkwardly, half-heartedly patting his back. "I know, Daddy," she murmured, her voice hollow. "It's okay."

(12) She led him gently to the couch and helped him sit. He clicked on the late show and settled into a subdued stupor. Megan crept upstairs and washed her battered face. She changed into a clean t-shirt and shorts and went back to the living room.

(13) "I'm going running," she announced, grabbing her house key from the table.

(14) He nodded silently. Then he glanced up. "Do me a favor before you go, Meggie-May?"

(15) "What do you need, Daddy?" she asked, knowing what he would ask for.

(16) "Bring me a beer, darling," he said with a wink.

(17) She brought him a frosty can, drowning in condensation. He took it and thanked her. Then he was lost in the eerie glow of the TV again, and Megan slipped out into the night.

(18) The cool summer breeze assaulted her senses, clearing the fog of pain and fear and anger and guilt. Her feet pattered, then pounded, then pummeled the pavement. She left the crumbling brownstone—and her crumbling life—far behind.

(19) She ran with the wind in her face and reality at her back. Running was freedom. Her aching, throbbing body loosened. Tears stung her eyes, and she submitted to the solace of sorrow. The empty streets embraced her. This was her escape.

(20) She ran for miles, past tall tenements that stretched concrete fingers toward the moon. She ran across a rust-speckled bridge, glancing down at the silent, slumbering, still depths of the river below. Across the river, larger houses sprawled on the banks. A few windows still glowed, but most were blank with darkness.

(21) It was time to go home. She knew it, even as every fiber of her body resisted. Winding her way back through silent neighborhoods, she pushed her body harder, gasping for air and aching for rest. As the streets grew darker and narrower, reality began to close again around her heart. The freedom and release gave way to fear, and she climbed the brownstone's dirty steps.

(22) Inside, the air was stale and thick. Megan's eyes adjusted to the glare of the TV, and she saw him, sprawled on the couch. She picked up the empty beer can that dangled from his limp fingers and took it to the kitchen. When she came back, she pulled a blanket loosely over him. He stirred in his sleep, nestling into the blanket. His eyes opened halfway.

(23) "Night, Meggie-May," he murmured, turning over to face the couch.

(24) Megan turned off the TV and started up the stairs. Halfway up, she stopped and looked down. Shadows danced across his features. He looked peaceful, helpless, deceptively harmless. She loved him and hated him in one tangled surge of emotion.

(25) "Goodnight, Daddy," she whispered to the darkness. Then she turned and went upstairs.

6. What do the misspelled words in paragraph 2 indicate?

Ⓐ The author's ignorance

Ⓑ The unusual dialect

Ⓒ A misprint in the text

Ⓓ The father's intoxication

7. Which of the following paragraphs clearly indicates that the physical abuse by Megan's father is a common occurrence?

Ⓐ Paragraph 6

Ⓑ Paragraph 7

Ⓒ Paragraph 9

Ⓓ Paragraph 10

8. Why is this story set late at night in dark settings?

Ⓐ People generally drink more at night

Ⓑ Running at night is safer

Ⓒ It illustrates the darkness of Megan's life

Ⓓ The setting is coincidental

9. Why does paragraph 21 say "every fiber of her body resisted" going home?

Ⓐ She enjoyed running and wanted to run more

Ⓑ Running was a freedom from her troubled life

Ⓒ She was afraid her father might be asleep

Ⓓ The route back home was mostly uphill

10. Which paragraph best describes Megan's feelings toward her father?

Ⓐ Paragraph 11

Ⓑ Paragraph 18

Ⓒ Paragraph 21

Ⓓ Paragraph 24

Questions 11 – 14 pertain to both "Caged" and "Freedom Run":

11. What symbol of depression and trouble is used in both of these pieces?

Ⓐ Metal bars

Ⓑ Physical abuse

Ⓒ Darkness

Ⓓ Dungeons

12. What strong desire do Megan and the narrator of "Caged" have in common?

Ⓐ Strength

Ⓑ Freedom

Ⓒ Light

Ⓓ Companionship

13. Which of the following emotions best describes the state of mind of Megan and the narrator of "Caged" at the end of the passages?

Ⓐ Hopelessness

Ⓑ Confidence

Ⓒ Joy

Ⓓ Anger

- 63 -

14. Which of the following is the key difference between Megan and the narrator of "Caged"?

Ⓐ Megan is a female; the narrator is a male

Ⓑ Megan is young; the narrator is old

Ⓒ Megan is hopeless; the narrator is hopeful

Ⓓ Megan is a victim; the narrator is a product of choices

Short Answer Question #1

What point of view is used in these passages? How does the point of view affect the power and meaning of each of these passages? Support your answer from the texts.

Questions 15 – 26 pertain to the following story:

The Top Five Reasons Video Games Are Good for Your Health

(1) Too many people think video games are just time-wasters. They say video games are for weak-minded imbeciles. They insist that no good can come from this electronic entertainment. In contrast to these common theories, I believe video games offer numerous benefits. Let me share with you the top five reasons that video games are good for your health.

(2) First, video games improve overall coordination. Response times are quicker, attention is more focused, and awareness is heightened. When I play video games, I find myself focused and intent on my mission. Since I began playing video games, my coordination—particularly my hand-eye coordination—has improved immensely. The results are obvious in many areas of my life, from cooking to driving to sports. Even my handwriting has improved! The advent of motion sensor systems (such as Nintendo's Wii, Microsoft's Xbox 360 Kinect, and Sony's PlayStation 3 Move) has further enhanced users' coordination and reaction times.

(3) In addition to improving coordination and reaction times, many games also enhance logic and reasoning abilities. Most games employ some sort of strategy, whether in sporting competitions, driving pursuits, fantasy quests, or military battles. Winning a game—even just playing a game—requires a plan and the ability to adjust that plan and adapt to changing conditions. The ability to use logic and reason to solve problems leads to the ability to think on your feet. These are all important life skills, making video games beneficial for personal development.

(4) Sometimes, however, you are not concerned about developing new skills—you just want to have fun. Video games are a great way to fill empty hours productively. They focus mental energies and allow unbridled relaxation. They entertain small children and keep older ones out of trouble. Finally, video games allow safe and fun experimentation in a variety of environments, with a plethora of tools, at a relatively low cost.

(5) Beyond creating skills and filling the hours with fun, video games also create a sense of passion and excitement. They encourage goal setting and persistence. They develop a healthy spirit of competition. When you play a

- 64 -

game often, you develop a deep desire to accomplish a little more or go a little further each time you play. This breeds excitement, anticipation, and a constant hope for success. Setting incremental goals and working passionately toward those goals leads to achievement in video games and in life.

(6) Finally, the skills and attitudes gained playing video games often open the door for development of deep social bonds. There is a unique camaraderie among those who play games together, almost as if they were teammates. These bonds tend to be strongest when a common game is played or when individuals are members of an online community. Even without these commonalities, however, the shared universe of video games provides the foundation for social interaction, conversation, and friendship.

(7) Are video games without pitfalls? Certainly not. But many games offer life-improving benefits that are often overlooked. They improve coordination and response time. They enhance logic and reasoning. They fill empty hours productively and create a sense of passion and excitement. Lastly, video games foster a variety of social bonds among players of all types, skill levels, and backgrounds. With so many positive aspects, video games are worth checking out. Try them—you might find you like them!

15. Which of the following is the best synonym for the word "imbecile" as it is used in paragraph 1?

Ⓐ Expert

Ⓑ Student

Ⓒ Fool

Ⓓ Child

16. Which of the following is not listed in this article as a primary benefit of video games?

Ⓐ They develop coordination

Ⓑ They enhance literacy

Ⓒ They create a sense of passion

Ⓓ They build social connections

17. What does the word "plethora" mean in paragraph 4?

Ⓐ A wide variety

Ⓑ A whole lot

Ⓒ Positive and negative

Ⓓ A few

18. What genre best describes this article?

Ⓐ Fiction

Ⓑ Memoir

Ⓒ Informational

Ⓓ Persuasive

19. Which paragraph presents personal examples to help illustrate the main idea of the paragraph?

Ⓐ Paragraph 1

Ⓑ Paragraph 2

Ⓒ Paragraph 5

Ⓓ Paragraph 6

20. What is the greatest weakness of the argument in this article?

Ⓐ It is poorly written

Ⓑ It is too brief

Ⓒ It is illogical

Ⓓ It offers no facts or statistics

21. What is the main idea of paragraph 4?

Ⓐ Video games fill empty hours with fun

Ⓑ Video games create a sense of passion

Ⓒ Video games help develop new skills

Ⓓ Video games develop social bonds

22. What does the author say has further enhanced users' coordination and reaction times?

Ⓐ More complex games

Ⓑ More complex controllers

Ⓒ Motion sensor systems

Ⓓ Increased game variety

- 66 -

23. What is the overall theme of this article?

Ⓐ Video games offer their users a number of benefits

Ⓑ Video games are powerful social tools

Ⓒ Many people think video games are time-wasters

Ⓓ Video games are not without pitfalls

24. Which of the following is a critique rather than a summary of this article?

Ⓐ This article takes a look at the benefits of video games

Ⓑ This piece identifies five positive effects of video games

Ⓒ With a sarcastic tone, this article ineffectively champions video games

Ⓓ Through opinion and experience, the author discusses video games

25. What is the most likely reason the author chose to list coordination development as the first benefit in this article?

Ⓐ It was the first benefit the author thought of

Ⓑ The author felt it would be the most persuasive thought

Ⓒ The benefits are listed in alphabetical order

Ⓓ There is no reason the author put that benefit first

26. Which of the following best summarizes paragraph 7?

Ⓐ Video games are good for everyone

Ⓑ Video games have a number of pitfalls

Ⓒ Social bonds are one of the greatest benefits of video games

Ⓓ Despite the pitfalls, video games are worth trying

Questions 27 – 38 pertain to the following story:

Hurricane

(1) The gentle winds that had toyed with the summer leaves were angrier by afternoon, going from playful to punishing. The cotton-ball clouds gathered into a slate-colored blanket, giving the world a dim, bluish cast. Hot, humid air hung heavily on branches and rooftops and hillsides. Breathing was a task; walking was a chore.

(2) Despite the impending storm, the little city center was alive with frantic bustle. Store shelves were cleared. Propane tanks were emptied in an army of cylinders. Cars were top-heavy with plywood and corrugated zinc. Restaurants and shops boarded their windows and locked their doors. The hurricane would roll in by nightfall, and no one wanted to be caught unprepared.

- 67 -

(3) Overlooking a deep gully two miles out of town, a little blue concrete house perched on a hilltop. Activity swirled around the house with the strengthening wind and gathering dusk. The house had seen many hurricanes in its long years on the hill, but none as broad and strong as this one was forecast to be.

(4) "Careful nuh, Adrian," Mimi called to her older brother. "Mi nah want yu fi fall."

(5) Adrian grinned down at her. He swung his lithe, lanky body across the rooftop, pausing to add another nail to the rickety zinc.

(6) "Mi nah gwine fall, Mimi," he promised. "Mi holding to dis yah roof like a likkle lizard."

(7) Mimi laughed and hurried back inside. Mama had dinner on the stove and she was busy stuffing the cracks around the kitchen window with old towels and scraps of cloth. The wooden slat windows around the house were all cranked shut, making the rooms dark and stale. In the front room and bedroom, Fitzroy moved beds and chairs away from the closed windows. The little boys had gone for water from the spring. Each member of the family knew exactly what to do.

(8) Mimi stirred the stewed beef and red peas bubbling on the old gas stove. Then she went to help Fitzroy. When the boys came back with the water and Adrian came down from the roof, they gathered for dinner. Plates of steaming beans and rice nearly covered the small, splintered tabletop. In the center, the flame of the kerosene lamp flickered and danced, casting unstable shadows around the room. From the shelf in the corner, a battery-powered radio squawked the latest news: the leading edge of the storm had already hit the southeastern tip of the island.

(9) An hour later, when the dishes were done and the zinc began to lift and shudder, the radio station was knocked off the air. A steady rain was falling, drumming evenly on the roof. Curious, Fitzroy opened the front door a crack and peered out. In the moonless night, the coconut palms were barely visible, bobbing and weaving like ghostly shadows in the brutal winds.

(10) "Fitzroy, shut di door, mon! Yu crazy?" Adrian pulled Fitzroy away from the door and shut it securely.

(11) They lounged on the beds and in chairs around the big room, reading or drawing or daydreaming in the dim light. The little boys played dominoes on the floor. The drumming of rain became a steady thunder and then a deafening roar. Wind slammed into the house, tearing at the straining roof panels and driving rain through the nail holes and window cracks. Each time a new leak appeared, they rearranged the furniture in a feeble attempt to keep things dry.

(12) Late in the night, Mama herded them to their beds and blew out the lamp. The boys piled noisily into the beds in their room. Mimi and Mama settled into the big bed in the front room. Inside, the house was silent, restful; but outside, the storm howled and raged like a petulant child, furiously flinging debris at the little blue house. Mimi was sure she could not and would not sleep. But she must have fallen asleep in spite of her fears, because she was awakened in the wee morning hours by the startling splash of water pelting her cheeks.

(13) Mimi sat up, groggy and disoriented. Mama was gone. Mimi could hear her in the bedroom, rousing the older boys to help move the big bed away

- 68 -

from a gaping hole in the roof. Mimi slipped from bed and began pulling off the soggy blankets. The rain was lighter now, and the wind was just a whisper. A few beams of wayward moonlight drifted through the open roof. Mama came back with the big boys and lit the lamp.

(14) Adrian was dressed. He helped move the bed, then opened the front door. The air was thick and nearly still. Adrian disappeared into the darkness. Minutes later, he reappeared in the empty space above them. When he grinned, his teeth gleamed in the lamplight.

(15) "Be careful nuh, Adrian," Mama warned. "It mus' be slick up der. Hurry with di work before di storm starts up again."

(16) Adrian nodded and disappeared again. A new piece of zinc crashed down over the hole, and Adrian pounded a handful of nails into the crosspieces.

(17) "Di storm not over, Mama?" Mimi asked. "It seems so nice an' calm."

(18) "Only di first half over," Mama explained. "Di second half will start soon. An' dat one der is mos' times di stronger part."

(19) Mimi shuddered and swallowed hard as her heart sank. She wished for daylight, for sunshine, for real calm. She wished the second half of the storm could pass them by. She hated the darkness, the wind, the rain, the fear. She hated the uncertainty and the waiting. She hated the hurricane.

(20) Mimi sat stiffly in a cane-back chair as Adrian finished the roof. When he was done, he came back in, wet and weary. The boys went back to bed and Mama stood beside Mimi.

(21) "Yu best come back to bed," Mama said gently, placing her hand on Mimi's shoulder. "Di eye of di storm won't last long. We mus' rest while we can."

(22) Mama blew out the lamp and plunged the room back into darkness. She led Mimi reluctantly back to the big bed. They settled into the fresh, dry blankets. Moments later, Mama was sleeping, her light, wheezing snore coming regularly through the ebony silence. Mimi resisted sleep. Her eyelids were heavy, but her mind was buzzing with fear. What if the whole roof came off? What if the hillside beneath them slid into the gully, carrying the little blue house with it? What if the royal palms behind the house fell on them? What if . . .?

(23) The fear remained unfinished as sleep claimed her. And as her psyche submitted to slumber, the winds began to whip around the little house once more.

27. What is the connotation of the metaphor "cotton-ball clouds" in paragraph 1?

Ⓐ Small and round

Ⓑ Thin and stringy

● White and fluffy

Ⓓ Fuzzy around the edges

28. Which paragraph indicates that this story is set on an island?

   Ⓐ Paragraph 2

   Ⓑ Paragraph 8

   Ⓒ Paragraph 9

   Ⓓ Paragraph 11

29. What is the implication in paragraph 9 when the author writes "the zinc began to lift and shudder"?

   Ⓐ Someone was on the roof

   Ⓑ The zinc was too loose

   Ⓒ Zinc is a poor roofing material

   Ⓓ The winds were picking up

30. Why does the author use dialect in this piece?

   Ⓐ It enhances the cultural setting of the story

   Ⓑ The author doesn't know how to spell properly

   Ⓒ It is a requirement for strong literary pieces

   Ⓓ It enhances the historical setting of the story

31. What point of view is used in this story?

   Ⓐ First person

   Ⓑ Second person

   Ⓒ Third person

   Ⓓ A and C

32. In paragraph 11, what literary devices are used?

   Ⓐ Personification

   Ⓑ Simile and paradox

   Ⓒ Personification and irony

   Ⓓ Simile

- 70 -

33. What word best describes the setting depicted in paragraph 2?

Ⓐ Relaxed

Ⓑ Excited

Ⓒ Angry

Ⓓ Busy

34. Why does the author use personification and metaphor in paragraph 1?

Ⓐ These devices add literary flair

Ⓑ These devices energize the setting descriptions

Ⓒ There is no particular reason

Ⓓ There is no other way to describe things

35. What is Mimi's attitude toward the second half of the hurricane?

Ⓐ Excitement

Ⓑ Indifference

Ⓒ Anxiety

Ⓓ Fatigue

36. Based on the information presented in this story, what is the eye of a hurricane?

Ⓐ The center

Ⓑ The leading edge

Ⓒ The back edge

Ⓓ The worst part

37. Based on the story, how would you describe Adrian's role in the family?

Ⓐ He shies away from work

Ⓑ He cares for the family

Ⓒ He is the youngest brother

Ⓓ He is a prankster

- 71 -

38. Considering the dialect, setting descriptions, and other clues in the text, where does this story most likely take place?

Ⓐ A coastal country in Africa

Ⓑ An island in the South Pacific

Ⓒ A coastal country in South America

Ⓓ An island in the Caribbean

Short Answer Question #2

Choose one character from this story and describe him or her in detail, focusing on two or three key character traits. Use evidence from the text to support your ideas.

Writing Test

Composition Prompt #1 – Expository Composition

Choose a current social problem about which you feel strongly. How would you resolve this social issue? Identify a specific potential solution and explain your solution in a well-developed essay.

Composition Prompt #2 – Literary Composition

Imagine you are receiving an award at an international symposium. What award are you receiving? Why? What are the presenters saying about your work? Tell about your experience.

Questions 39 – 48 pertain to the following procedural essay:

How to Bake Beautiful Brownies

(1) Who doesn't love brownies. (2) For decades, this decadent dessert has been a favorite. (3) While some cooks still craft brownies from starch, there are many mixes available that produce perfect, chewy, chocolaty brownies. (4) In fact, with the help of a mix, you can bake beautiful brownies in three simple steps.
(5) The first step in baking beautiful brownies is preparing your tools and ingredients. (6) You will need a large mixing bowl, a sturdy mixing spoon, and a properly-sized baking pan. (7) You will also need cooking spray and, of course, the brownie mix and the ingredients listed on the package. (8) Spray the bottom of the baking pan with the cooking spray, and preheat the oven to 350 degrees Fahrenheit. (9) When you have assembled and prepared everything, your ready to start mixing.
(10) The second step in baking beautiful brownies is making the batter. (11) Next, add the oil, water, and eggs as directed on the package. (12) Dump the

- 72 -

brownie mix into your mixing bowl. (13) Using the sturdy spoon, mix the batter approximately 50 strokes, or until everything is well-moistened. (14) When the batter is ready, pour it into the pan, smoothing the top with the back of the mixing spoon. (15) Finally, your brownies are ready to go into the oven.

(16) The last step in baking beautiful brownies is the actual baking. (17) Place the pan in the oven and set a timer for the appropriate time listed on the brownie mix packaging. (18) It is a good idea to check the brownies too or three minutes before the baking time is up to prevent over-baking. (19) When a toothpick inserted two inches from the edge of the pan comes out with moist crumbs on it the brownies are done. (20) Remove the brownies from the oven, and place them on a rack to cool.

(21) When the brownies are cool, cute them to the desired size. (22) Using a plastic knife to cut the brownies. (23) This will prevent tearing and create smooth cut lines. (24) Now, there's only one thing left to do—enjoy your beautifully-baked brownies. (25) You deserve them!

39. In sentence 1, what change, if any, needs to be made?

Ⓐ No change is needed.

🅑 Change the period to a question mark

Ⓒ Change the period to an exclamation point

Ⓓ Change the period to a comma

40. What change, if any, is necessary to improve the meaning and clarity of sentence 3?

Ⓐ No change is necessary.

Ⓑ Remove the comma after starch

Ⓒ Change craft to crave

🅓 Change starch to scratch

41. Which sentence functions as the thesis of this essay?

🅐 Sentence 2

Ⓑ Sentence 3

🅒 Sentence 4

Ⓓ Sentence 5

42. What change, if any, needs to be made in sentence 6?

Ⓐ No change is necessary

Ⓑ Add a colon after need

Ⓒ Remove the comma after spoon

Ⓓ Insert a comma between sturdy and mixing

43. What is the problem with sentence 9?

Ⓐ Have should be had

Ⓑ Your should be you're

Ⓒ There should not be a comma after everything

Ⓓ Everything should be every thing

44. How could the sentence order be improved in the third paragraph?

Ⓐ Switch sentences 11 and 12

Ⓑ Switch sentences 13 and 14

Ⓒ Switch sentences 12 and 13

Ⓓ Switch sentences 14 and 15

45. What change, if any, is needed in sentence 18?

Ⓐ No change is needed.

Ⓑ Change too to two

Ⓒ Change three to 3

Ⓓ Insert a comma after up

46. What punctuation change is most appropriate in sentence 19?

Ⓐ No change is needed.

Ⓑ Insert a comma after out and a comma after it

Ⓒ Insert a comma after it

Ⓓ Replace the period with an exclamation point

- 74 -

47. What change, if any, is needed in sentence 21?

Ⓐ No change is needed.

Ⓑ Remove the comma after cool

Ⓒ Change to to into

Ⓓ Change cute to cut

48. How would you classify the problem with sentence 22?

Ⓐ It is a gerund phrase, not a sentence

Ⓑ It is an infinitive phrase, not a sentence

Ⓒ It is a comma splice, not a sentence

Ⓓ There is no error in sentence 22

Questions 49 – 58 pertain to the following essay:

Road Trip

(1) Nothing says Summer like a family road trip. (2) There's just something about the sweaty, sweltering hours in a crowded car that makes each road trip seem like a memorable—if misguided—adventure. (3) I've been on several roadtrips in my life, and each one had its own special charm. (4) Above all other road trips, however, I will always remember my family trip to the Grand Canyon when I was twelve years old.

(5) The day we left was bright and cloudless. (6) I squeezed into the backseat between my little brother, Ronnie, and my big sister, Rebecca. (7) We piled the ingredients of a successful road trip around us, sodas, snacks, music, and games. (8) By the time we hit the freeway—a mere seven miles from our house—Ronnie and I had each already downed a whole soda and were starting on a second one, we were also halfway through a bag of chips. (9) What can I say? (10) We were growing boys. (11) Needless to say, we begged to stop at every rest area along the route, driving my father crazy. (12) Another thing that drove my father memorably crazy was our road games. (13) Twenty minutes into our drive, Rebecca began the alphabet game. (14) We start with the letter A, and each time one of us saw the next letter of the alphabet, we shouted it out. (15) There were long periods of silence as we watched road signs and license plates intently. (16) Then, when a letter appeared, we would all burst out shouting, and my startled father would swerve in surprise and yell at us to keep the noise down. (17) The alphabet game was a source of grate amusement and a handful of fistfights during that never-ending trip.

(18) The trip wasn't all fun and games, however. (19) In fact, we had several disasters on our journey. (20) In retrospect, our challenges seem almost funny, but at the time, they seemed tragic. (21) We blue a tire on a lonely, dusty stretch of highway in triple-digit temperatures. (22) We caught some fish in a tiny, lakeside campground just across the Arizona border, but Mom turned our fish to charcoal over the campfire. (23) When we finally made it to the Grand Canyon, Rebecca fell on a rocky trail and broke her ankle. (24)

- 75 -

We spent the rest of the trip in a dimly-lit hotel room, playing cards and watching movies so Rebecca wouldn't feel left out.

(25) Looking back, I'm sure it wasn't the trip my parents had planned for it to be. (26) But it was a trip I will never forget. (27) It was the imperfections that made the trip so memorable. (28) By the time we got home, we all hated each other a little and loved each other a lot.

49. What change, if any, needs to be made in sentence 1?

Ⓐ No change is needed.

Ⓑ Change says to say

Ⓒ Change Summer to summer

Ⓓ Change road trip to roadtrip

50. In sentence 3, what change is most appropriate?

Ⓐ Change roadtrips to road trips

Ⓑ Change been to being

Ⓒ Change had to has

Ⓓ Sentence 3 is correct as it is written.

51. Which sentence in paragraph 1 functions as the thesis of this essay?

Ⓐ Sentence 1

Ⓑ Sentence 2

Ⓒ Sentence 3

Ⓓ Sentence 4

52. How can the punctuation error in sentence 7 be corrected?

Ⓐ Insert commas after ingredients and trip

Ⓑ Change the comma after us to a colon

Ⓒ Change the comma after us to a semicolon

Ⓓ Remove the comma after music

53. What is the problem with sentence 8?

&#9off; Ⓐ There is no problem with sentence 8

Ⓑ Sentence 8 is a sentence fragment

🅒 Sentence 8 is a comma splice

Ⓓ Sentence 8 has a misused infinitive phrase

54. What correction, if any, is needed in sentence 14?

Ⓐ No correction is needed

🅑 Change start to started

Ⓒ Change saw to see

Ⓓ Change shouted to shout

55. In sentence 17, what change is most appropriate?

🅐 Change grate to great

Ⓑ Change handful to hand full

Ⓒ Change fistfights to fist fights

Ⓓ Change never-ending to never ending

56. What change, if any, should be made in sentence 21?

Ⓐ No change is necessary.

🅑 Change blue to blew

Ⓒ Change highway to high-way

Ⓓ Change triple-digit to triple digit

57. In sentence 23, which of the following is the most appropriate correction?

Ⓐ Remove the comma after Canyon

Ⓑ Insert a comma after trail

Ⓒ Insert a comma after it

🅓 Sentence 23 is correct as it is written

58. Which of the following sentences would make the best concluding sentence for this essay?

(A) The alphabet game was the best part of all

(B) In the end, it would have been more enjoyable if we had not blown a tire and Rebecca had not broken her ankle

(C) The challenges we faced and the unexpected experiences made our Grand Canyon adventure the most memorable trip ever

(D) I feel blessed to have such an adventurous family

Questions 59 – 68 pertain to the following essay:

A Brief History of Basketball

(1) Basketball is, arguably, one of the most popular and most exciting sports of our time. (2) Behind this fast-paced sport, however, is a rich history. (3) There has been many changes made to the game over the years, but the essence remains the same. (4) From it's humble beginnings in 1891, basketball has grown to have worldwide appeal.

(5) One thing that sets the history of basketball apart from other major sports is the fact that it was created by just one man. (6) In 1891, Dr. James Naismith, a teacher and Presbyterian Minister, needed an indoor game to keep college students at the Springfield, Massachusetts YMCA Training School busy during long winter days. (7) This need prompted the creation of basketball, which was originally played by tossing a soccer ball into an empty peach basket nailed to the gym wall. (8) There was two teams, but only one basket in the original game.

(9) Dr. Naismith's YMCA game became so popular that teams began to form throughout the New England region. (10) Early games among these teams were rough and rowdy. (11) In fact, the games were generally played in steel or chicken-wire cages players often became injured when they crashed into these cages. (12) Over time, the metal cages were replaced by rope-mesh cages, reducing injuries and making basketball a more enjoyable game for the players.

(13) Just as the equipment for the game of basketball has changed over time the rules have changed as well. (14) The original game, as it was invented by Dr. Naismith, had only 13 rules written on two pages. (15) In contrast, the modern rulebook has more than 60 pages of rules! (16) Despite the increase in rules, the basics of basketball have not changed in more than a century, making it relatively simple to learn and play.

(17) Because of the simplicity of basketball, the game had spread across the nation within 30 years of its invention in Massachusetts. (18) As more teams formed, the need for a league became apparent. (19) The smaller National Basketball League (NBL) formed soon after. (20) On June 6, 1946, the Basketball Association of America (BAA) was formed. (21) In 1948, the BAA absconded the NBL, and the National Basketball Association (NBA) was born. (22) The NBA played its first full season in 1948-49 and is still going strong today.

(23) Though much has changed in our world since 1891, the popularity of the sport of basketball has remained strong. (24) From it's humble start in a

YMCA gym to the multi-million-dollar empire it is today, the simple fun of the sport has endured. (25) Although many changes have been made over the years, the essence of basketball has remained constant. (26) Its rich history and simplicity ensure that basketball will always be a popular sport around the world.

59. What correction, if any, needs to be made in sentence 1?

   Ⓐ No correction is needed.

   Ⓑ Remove the comma after arguably

   Ⓒ Remove both commas

   Ⓓ Insert a comma after popular

60. In sentence 3, what change is most appropriate?

   Ⓐ Remove the comma

   Ⓑ Change has to have

   Ⓒ Change been to being

   Ⓓ Sentence 3 is correct as it is written

61. How would you correct sentence 4 in this essay?

   Ⓐ Change beginnings to beginning

   Ⓑ Change worldwide to world-wide

   Ⓒ Change has to had

   Ⓓ Change it's to its

62. What type of error is found in sentence 6?

   Ⓐ Punctuation error

   Ⓑ Wording error

   Ⓒ Capitalization error

   Ⓓ There is not an error in sentence 6

63. What correction, if any, is necessary in sentence 8?

   Ⓐ No correction is necessary

   Ⓑ Change was to were

   Ⓒ Write the numbers as numerals instead of words

   Ⓓ Remove the comma

64. What is the problem with sentence 11?

Ⓐ It is a run-on sentence

Ⓑ It is a comma splice

Ⓒ It is a sentence fragment

Ⓓ Sentence 11 is correct as it is written

65. What change, if any, is needed in sentence 13?

Ⓐ No change is needed

Ⓑ Insert a comma after equipment

Ⓒ Insert a comma after time

Ⓓ Insert a comma after changed

66. Which of the following changes would most improve the organization and clarity of paragraph 5 of this essay?

Ⓐ The paragraph is correct as it is written

Ⓑ Move sentence 18 to the beginning of the paragraph

Ⓒ Switch sentences 19 and 20

Ⓓ Switch sentences 21 and 22

67. Which of the following words would best replace the misused word absconded in sentence 21?

Ⓐ Appropriated

Ⓑ Ascended

Ⓒ Aborted

Ⓓ Absorbed

68. What change, if any, is needed in sentence 24?

Ⓐ No change is needed

Ⓑ Change it's to its

Ⓒ Remove the hyphens from multi-million-dollar

Ⓓ Remove the comma after today

- 80 -

Answers and Explanations

TEKS Standard §110.31(b)(1)(B)

1. C: is the best choice because the connotation of the word "dungeon" is that the narrator's life is dark and unrelenting. The reason A is wrong is that the other details in the poem that precede line 8 (being caged, and surrounded by metal bars, having only one hour of being outdoors a day), wouldn't apply to someone living in the basement of a castle.

TEKS Standard §110.31(b)(3)

2. A: "Caged" is set in a prison. Although this fact is never explicitly stated anywhere in the poem, no other interpretation is possible. The author is caged, surrounded by metal bars, led around by authority figures, and allowed outdoors only once a day. Even when he is outdoors, he is still surrounded by chain link fences and barbed wired, and he is filled with despair and hopelessness.

TEKS Standard §110.31(b)(3)

3. D: Alliteration is used throughout the poem to underscore the repetitive nature of the narrator's life. Alliteration involves using words that share the same beginning sounds. Examples of this in the poem can be found in lines 2, 7, 9, 18, 27, and 28.

TEKS Standard §110.31(b)(3) and (5)(C)

4. A: is the best choice because this poem is written using first-person point of view. That is, the story is told from the point of view of the subject, the prisoner. Had the second person point of view been used, instead of "I", the author would have used "you" to refer to the subject of the poem. Had it been written in the third person, the subject of the poem would be "he" or "the prisoner", or the prisoner's name.

TEKS Standard §110.31(b)(3)(A) and (7)

5. B: is the best choice because lines 18-22 reference the narrator's desire for a fresh start. He talks about being "cleansed", or putting his past and his bad deeds behind him, and says that every time he comes outside hope wells up inside him, only to be dashed when the guards come to take him back to his cell.

TEKS Standard §110.31(b)(5)(B) and Figure: 19 TAC §110.30(b)(110.31)(B)

6. D: The misspelled words in paragraph 2 indicate slurred speech caused by the father's intoxication.

TEKS Standard §110.31(b)(5)(A) and Figure: 19 TAC §110.30(b)(110.31)(B)

7. A: Paragraph 6 clearly shows that the physical abuse by Megan's father is a common occurrence with this sentence: "She had learned long ago that backing away only prolonged the misery."

TEKS Standard §110.31(b)(5) and Figure: 19 TAC §110.30(b)(110.31)(B)

8. C: "Freedom Run" is set late at night in dark settings to illustrate the darkness that her father's drunkenness and physical abuse creates in Megan's life.

TEKS Standard §110.31(b)(5) and Figure: 19 TAC §110.30(b)(110.31)(B)
9. B: is the best choice because paragraph 21 is meant to indicate that Megan did not want to go home because running represents freedom from her troubled life.

TEKS Standard §110.31(b)(5) and Figure: 19 TAC §110.30(b)(110.31)(B)
10. D: Paragraph 24 is the portion of the story that best describes Megan's feelings toward her father. The author makes it clear that the abuse has caused Megan to develop a love/hate relationship with her father.

TEKS Standard §110.31(b)(7)
11. C: Darkness is the symbol of depression and trouble that is used in both pieces.

TEKS Standard §110.31(b)(2)
12. B: Megan and the narrator of "Caged" both strongly desire freedom, one from incarceration, and the other from physical abuse at the hands of her drunken father.

TEKS Standard §110.31(b)(2)
13. A: Both Megan and the narrator of "Caged" demonstrate a sense of hopelessness at the end. With the unnamed prisoner, this is expressed explicitly. His hopes for a new beginning are crushed every day when the guards return him to his prison cell, where he will face 23 more hours of despair. Megan's hopelessness is not as clear, but by not showing any indication of real change on the part of her father, the author clearly implies that Megan's life will be much the same tomorrow night, and every night for the foreseeable future.

TEKS Standard §110.31(b)(5)
14. D: Megan is a victim through no fault of her own. She has done nothing to deserve the violent physical attacks by her father, while the man in the poem is suffering in prison because of his own actions in the past.

Sample Short Answer #1

> "Caged" is written in first-person point of view. This gives the reader an inside perspective on what the narrator is thinking and feeling. With the use of the first-person pronoun "I," the reader feels intimately connected to the narrator, increasing the power of the passage.
>
> In contrast to "Caged," "Freedom Run" is written in third-person point of view. This gives the reader a broad perspective on Megan's life and her situation. It also allows the author to include details that could not be included in first-person writing. This increases the power of the writing by making it more objective.

TEKS Standard §110.31(b)(1)(A)
15. C: The word "imbecile" is used as an insult; it means a very stupid person. The word "fool" means pretty much the same thing.

TEKS Standard §110.31(b)(10)(A)
16. B: The article does not list enhanced literacy as a benefit of video games, but it does list all the benefits found in the other answer choices.

- 82 -

TEKS Standard §110.31(b)(1)(A)

17. A: The noun "plethora" means "a wide variety."

TEKS Standard §110.31(b)(10) and (2)

18. D: This essay falls into the persuasive genre. The author is trying to persuade the reader that video games are actually good for one's health, contrary to widespread popular opinion.

TEKS Standard §110.31(b)(10)

19. B: Paragraphs 1, 5, and 6 do not use personal examples to illustrate the main ideas. Only Paragraph 2 does.

TEKS Standard §110.31(b)(10)(A)

20. D: The greatest weakness of this article is that it does not present facts or statistics to support its claims. A, B, and C do not reflect true weaknesses of the article. The article is lengthy enough for what it's trying to do, it's logical, and it's well written.

TEKS Standard §110.31(b)(10)

21. A: The main idea of paragraph 4 is that video games fill empty hours with fun. B, C, and D are not the best choices because they do not accurately represent the main idea of paragraph 4.

TEKS Standard §110.31(b)(10)

22. C: In paragraph 2, the author says that motion sensor systems have further enhanced users' coordination and reaction times.

TEKS Standard §110.31(b)(10) and (2)

23. A: The overall theme of the article is that video games offer a number of benefits.

TEKS Standard §110.31(b)(9)(A)

24. C offers an opinion-based critique of the article rather than a fact-based summary of the article. A, B, and D are all fact-based summaries rather than opinion-based critiques of the article.

TEKS Standard §110.31(b)(10)(A)

25. B most accurately reflects the reason that coordination development was listed as the first benefit in this article. The author says he is going to list the "top five" reasons video games are good for a person's health. Out of his five reasons, his first one, that video games improve coordination, is the most closely related to health. It's reasonable to assume that he therefore thinks it's the most important reason of the five.

TEKS Standard §110.31(b)(10)

26. D best summarizes the thoughts in paragraph 7, which is that video games are worth playing despite their pitfalls.

TEKS Standard §110.31(b)(1)(B)

27. C: Words can have both a denotation, which is their actual, literal meaning, and a connotation, which is the notion or feeling the word or phrase causes. "White and fluffy" are what most people would think of if they read the phrase "cotton ball clouds."

TEKS Standard §110.31(b)(5) and Figure: 19 TAC §110.30(b)(110.31)(B)
28. B: We know that this story takes place on an island, because it says so in paragraph 8: "the leading edge of the storm had already hit the southeastern tip of the island."

TEKS Standard §110.31(b)(1)(B)
29. D: The implication of "the zinc began to lift and shudder" in paragraph 9 is that the winds were picking up. The story indicates that people are using zinc to protect their homes from the winds, so when it begins to lift and shudder, it's a sign that the wind is getting even stronger.

TEKS Standard §110.31(b)(2)(C)
30. A: Dialect is used in this story to enhance the cultural setting of the story. By showing how the islanders actually speak, the author is adding authenticity to the story.

TEKS Standard §110.31(b)(5)
31. C: This story is written in third-person point of view. That means it's being told by a narrator, who does not have any part in the events. If it were written in the first-person, the story would be told by one of the main subjects, who would use personal pronouns such as "I", "we", "me", and "us."

TEKS Standard §110.31(b)(7)
32. A: When the author describes the rain as "drumming" in paragraph 11, this is an example of personification. Personification is attributing human actions or characteristics to inanimate things. Rain cannot play drums, but by employing this metaphor the author gives us an idea of how the rain sounded.

TEKS Standard §Figure: 19 TAC §110.30(b)(110.31)(B)
33. D: The setting depicted in paragraph 2 is best described as "busy." The opening sentence of the paragraph makes this clear: "Despite the impending storm, the little city center was alive with frantic bustle."

TEKS Standard §110.31(b)(7) and Figure: 19 TAC §110.30(b)(110.31)(B)
34. B: is the best choice because the personification and metaphor in paragraph 1 serve to energize the setting description; that is, they help bring the scene to life in the reader's mind.

TEKS Standard §110.31(b)(5) and Figure: 19 TAC §110.30(b)(110.31)(B)
35. C: Paragraph 19 makes it clear that Mimi's attitude toward the second half of the hurricane is anxiety.

TEKS Standard §110.31(b)(1)(B)
36. A: The text indicates that the eye of the hurricane is the center of the hurricane. It does so by showing the lull that develops between the first half of the hurricane, and the second half.

TEKS Standard §110.31(b)(5) and Figure: 19 TAC §110.30(b)(110.31)(B)
37. B: Throughout the story, Adrian works hard to help protect the family from the hurricane.

38. D: Based on the dialect, setting, and other clues in the text, this story likely takes place on an island in the Caribbean.

Sample Short Answer #2

Mimi is nurturing, caring deeply for her family. Her nurturing tendencies are seen in paragraph 4, when she cautions Adrian not to fall, and in paragraph 8, when Mimi stirs the dinner without being asked and then goes to help her brother. These passages—and others—clearly demonstrate her desire to help and care for others.

In addition to her nurturing qualities, Mimi also exhibits a great deal of anxiety. In paragraph 12, she has trouble falling asleep because of the storm. In paragraph 20, Mimi sits "stiffly" even in the calm eye of the storm, while paragraph 19 discusses her fear in the face of the second half of the storm. Finally, in paragraph 22, Mimi is once again unable to sleep because of anxiety, reiterating the anxious nature of her personality.

Sample Composition #1 – Expository Composition:
Triumph Through Training Programs

In our current economy, unemployment is a pressing issue. The unemployment numbers for young people, however, are up to 50 percent higher than those for experienced workers. Most young people are not adequately equipped to compete in the work world. This problem can be tackled through training programs designed to help young workers identify their interests, develop skills, and build a professional network.

First, training programs can help unemployed young people identify their interests. Many young workers are clueless about their professional passions and natural aptitudes. Training programs can help them identify these things and find areas in which they should develop. This will help young and inexperienced workers develop passion and motivation for their job search.

Once interests have been identified, training programs can help young workers develop skills in those areas of interest. More practical and focused than college courses, training programs can hone in on specific traits and abilities necessary for particular jobs or industries. Developing these skills can give young workers both confidence and a competitive edge over other job candidates.

With a list of interests and a wealth of new skills, young workers can also use training programs to build a professional network. Industry contacts are more necessary than ever before when conducting a job search. The old adage, "It's not what you know; it's who you know," has proven true for many job seekers. Training programs can help young workers build a professional network of contacts through special speakers, job fairs, internships, and other avenues.

Searching for a job is always daunting, but it can be especially intimidating for workers with little or no experience. Training programs can help ease these fears. They can help workers identify interests, develop skills, and build a professional network of contacts. With these tools—gained through training programs—young workers will be equipped to beat the unemployment obstacles and go out and find the job of their dreams.

Sample Composition #2 – Literary Composition:

Humanitarian of the Year

The crowd hushed as the Master of Ceremonies stepped to the microphone. He began with the story of Peter, a sickly young boy who was cured by my dietary discovery. Then he spoke of Kayla, a mother of two, who was on her deathbed before using my serum. He invited the now-healthy Kayla, who was in attendance, to stand and wave. The audience smiled and applauded enthusiastically.

With a sideways glance at me, the Master of Ceremonies announced, "And now, please welcome our Humanitarian of the Year!"

As he called my name, the audience rose to their feet, and I slipped from my velvet-padded chair. I approached the podium and shook hands with the Master of Ceremonies. He gave me an award certificate and a plaque. We posed for a picture before the still-applauding crowd.

"Please, say a few words," he said, motioning to the microphone.

I nodded and stepped to the microphone as the audience took their seats. The room was warm and bright with soft lights and candles. Thick velvet drapes swathed the walls gracefully. Black-coated waiters floated among the well-dressed symposium attendees, refilling coffee and water and silently clearing finished plates. Nearly every eye was on me. This was my moment.

"Thank you for the honor of this award," I began. "The journey to this podium started five years ago when my mother became desperately ill."

I went on to tell them of my struggle to find a natural cure for her ills. From that struggle was born the dietary serum that had changed so many lives and helped so many people. I thanked my family, my research assistants, my sponsors, and my supporters. Then I took my seat.

Throughout the night, people approached me to share their stories. It seemed that everyone knew someone who had been affected by my discoveries. I listened to each story with an overwhelming mixture of awe and pride. I felt honored to be the Humanitarian of the Year, but I felt even more honored to have the opportunity to touch so many lives with my life's dream.

TEKS Standard §110.31(b)(18)(B)

39. B: Sentence 1 is a question and needs a question mark as the end punctuation.

TEKS Standard §110.31(b)(13)(C) and (D)

40. D: In this sentence, "scratch" is a better word choice than "starch." As written, that part of the sentence makes no sense, but it makes perfect sense if we replace "starch" with "scratch."

TEKS Standard §110.31(b)(15)(A)(iii)

41. C: Sentence 4 functions as the thesis statement for this essay, clearly presenting the main idea of the entire piece, which is how to bake beautiful brownies. Generally, the thesis sentence of an article will have much in common with the article's title.

TEKS Standard §110.31(b)(13)
42. A: Sentence 6 is correct as written; no change is necessary.

TEKS Standard §110.31(b)(13)(D) and (19)
43. B: Changing "your" into "you're" is the appropriate correction for sentence 9. "Your" is a possessive pronoun, while "you're" is a contraction of "you are", which is what the author intended to say here.

TEKS Standard §110.31(b)(13)
44. A: Switching sentences 11 and 12 improves the order and clarity of the third paragraph by organizing the steps more chronologically. B, C, and D would actually further disrupt the chronological order of the paragraph.

TEKS Standard §110.31(b)(13)(C) and (13)(D) and (19)
45. B: The word "two" is the correct word for sentence 18, as the concept referenced is a number. The word "too" means also, besides, in addition to, etc.

TEKS Standard §110.31(b)(18)(B)(ii)
46. A: Sentence 19 is correct as written; no change is needed.

TEKS Standard §110.31(b)(13)(C) and (13)(D)
47. D: The word "cute" is either a misspelling, or a typographical error; it should be "cut."

TEKS Standard §110.31(b)(17)(A)(i)
48. A: Sentence 22 is a sentence fragment consisting of nothing but a gerund phrase. It cannot stand alone as a sentence.

TEKS Standard §110.31(b)(18)(A)
49. C: The word "summer" has been improperly capitalized in sentence 1. In ordinary usage, the names of the seasons should not be capitalized.

TEKS Standard §110.31(b)(13)(D)
50. A: The phrase "road trip" should always be written as two words, not one. This holds true for the plural form of the phrase as well.

TEKS Standard §110.31(b)(15)(A)(iii)
51. D: Sentence 4 functions as the thesis in this essay. It introduces the main point of the article, which is to describe the author's memorable road trip to the Grand Canyon as a child.

TEKS Standard §110.31(b)(18)(B)
52. B: Changing the comma to a colon corrects the error in sentence 7 and prepares the reader for the list of items that follows.

TEKS Standard §110.31(b)(18)
53. C: Sentence 8 is a comma splice, which is a type of run-on sentence. A period should come after "one", and "we were also halfway through a bag of chips" should be converted into a complete sentence that stands alone.

TEKS Standard §110.31(b)(17)(A)(i)

54. B converts the verb "start" into the proper past tense, "started." This matches the tense of not only the rest of the sentence, but also the rest of the article.

TEKS Standard §110.31(b)(13)(C) and (13)(D) and (19)

55. A: The word "grate" is incorrect; it should be "great." Either the author made a spelling error, or he confused two words that sound exactly alike, but have two different meanings – "grate" and "great."

TEKS Standard §110.31(b)(13)(C) and (13)(D) and (19)

56. B: The word "blue" is a color. It should be replaced with the word "blew", which is a verb.

TEKS Standard §110.31(b)(13)

57. D: Sentence 19 is correct as written; no change is needed.

TEKS Standard §110.31(b)(13)

58. C: This is the best choice for a concluding sentence, because it's about the entire story. The other choices don't focus on the story as a whole, but only smaller parts of it.

TEKS Standard §110.31(b)(18)(B)(2)

59. A: Sentence 1 is correct as it is written.

TEKS Standard §110.31(b)(17)(A)

60. B: Sentence 3 needs a plural verb "have been" in this clause, in order to match the plural subject of the clause, which is "changes."

TEKS Standard §110.31(b)(17)(A) and (18)(B)

61. D: The word "it's" in this sentence is used incorrectly, because it is a contraction of "it is", which makes no sense. The word should be "its", which is a possessive pronoun.

TEKS Standard §110.31(b)(18)(A)

62. C: Sentence 6 contains a capitalization error. The word "minister" should not be capitalized unless it's part of a title. In this instance, it's not part of a title, but is used as a job description.

TEKS Standard §110.31(b)(17)(A)(i)

63. B: In the first clause of sentence 8, "teams" is plural, so it must have a plural verb to go with it. So "was" needs to be changed to "were."

TEKS Standard §110.31(b)(13)(D)

64. A: Sentence 11 is a run-on sentence. It should be corrected by adding a semicolon after "cages."

TEKS Standard §110.31(b)(18)(B)(ii)

65. C: Adding a comma after time separates the introductory clause from the main clause of the sentence.

TEKS Standard §110.31(b)(13)

66. C: Switching sentences 19 and 20 improves the organization and clarity of paragraph 5.

TEKS Standard §110.31(b)(13)(C)

67. D: The word "absconded" means "went away secretly and in a hurry"; it makes no sense in this sentence. The word "absorbed" should replace it, to show that the two entities combined to form a single organization.

TEKS Standard §110.31(b)(13)(C)

68. B: The word "its" in this sentence is used incorrectly, because it is actually a possessive pronoun. The word needed is "it's", which is a contraction of "it is."

- 89 -

General Strategies

The most important thing you can do is to ignore your fears and jump into the test immediately- do not be overwhelmed by any strange-sounding terms. You have to jump into the test like jumping into a pool- all at once is the easiest way.

Make Predictions

As you read and understand the question, try to guess what the answer will be. Remember that several of the answer choices are wrong, and once you begin reading them, your mind will immediately become cluttered with answer choices designed to throw you off. Your mind is typically the most focused immediately after you have read the question and digested its contents. If you can, try to predict what the correct answer will be. You may be surprised at what you can predict.

Quickly scan the choices and see if your prediction is in the listed answer choices. If it is, then you can be quite confident that you have the right answer. It still won't hurt to check the other answer choices, but most of the time, you've got it!

Answer the Question

It may seem obvious to only pick answer choices that answer the question, but the test writers can create some excellent answer choices that are wrong. Don't pick an answer just because it sounds right, or you believe it to be true. It MUST answer the question. Once you've made your selection, always go back and check it against the question and make sure that you didn't misread the question, and the answer choice does answer the question posed.

Benchmark

After you read the first answer choice, decide if you think it sounds correct or not. If it doesn't, move on to the next answer choice. If it does, mentally mark that answer choice. This doesn't mean that you've definitely selected it as your answer choice, it just means that it's the best you've seen thus far. Go ahead and read the next choice. If the next choice is worse than the one you've already selected, keep going to the next answer choice. If the next choice is better than the choice you've already selected, mentally mark the new answer choice as your best guess.

The first answer choice that you select becomes your standard. Every other answer choice must be benchmarked against that standard. That choice is correct until proven otherwise by another answer choice beating it out. Once you've decided that no other answer choice seems as good, do one final check to ensure that your answer choice answers the question posed.

Valid Information

Don't discount any of the information provided in the question. Every piece of information may be necessary to determine the correct answer. None of the information in the question is there to throw you off (while the answer choices will certainly have information to throw you off). If two seemingly unrelated topics are discussed, don't ignore either. You can be confident there is a relationship, or it wouldn't be included in the question, and you are probably going to have to determine what is that relationship to find the answer.

Avoid "Fact Traps"

Don't get distracted by a choice that is factually true. Your search is for the answer that answers the question. Stay focused and don't fall for an answer that is true but incorrect. Always go back to the question and make sure you're choosing an answer that actually answers the question and is not just a true statement. An answer can be factually correct, but it MUST answer the question asked. Additionally, two answers can both be seemingly correct, so be sure to read all of the answer choices, and make sure that you get the one that BEST answers the question.

Milk the Question

Some of the questions may throw you completely off. They might deal with a subject you have not been exposed to, or one that you haven't reviewed in years. While your lack of knowledge about the subject will be a hindrance, the question itself can give you many clues that will help you find the correct answer. Read the question carefully and look for clues. Watch particularly for adjectives and nouns describing difficult terms or words that you don't recognize. Regardless of if you completely understand a word or not, replacing it with a synonym either provided or one you more familiar with may help you to understand what the questions are asking. Rather than wracking your mind about specific detailed information concerning a difficult term or word, try to use mental substitutes that are easier to understand.

The Trap of Familiarity

Don't just choose a word because you recognize it. On difficult questions, you may not recognize a number of words in the answer choices. The test writers don't put "make-believe" words on the test; so don't think that just because you only recognize all the words in one answer choice means that answer choice must be correct. If you only recognize words in one answer choice, then focus on that one. Is it correct? Try your best to determine if it is correct. If it is, that is great, but if it doesn't, eliminate it. Each word and answer choice you eliminate increases your chances of getting the question correct, even if you then have to guess among the unfamiliar choices.

Eliminate Answers

Eliminate choices as soon as you realize they are wrong. But be careful! Make sure you consider all of the possible answer choices. Just because one appears right, doesn't mean that the next one won't be even better! The test writers will usually put more than one good answer choice for every question, so read all of them. Don't worry if you are stuck between two that seem right. By getting down to just two remaining possible choices, your odds are now 50/50. Rather than wasting too much time, play the odds. You are guessing, but guessing wisely, because you've been able to knock out some of the answer choices that you know are wrong. If you are eliminating choices and realize that the last answer choice you are left with is also obviously wrong, don't panic. Start over and consider each choice again. There may easily be something that you missed the first time and will realize on the second pass.

Tough Questions

If you are stumped on a problem or it appears too hard or too difficult, don't waste time. Move on! Remember though, if you can quickly check for obviously incorrect answer choices, your chances of guessing correctly are greatly improved. Before you completely give up, at least try to knock out a couple of possible answers. Eliminate what you can and then guess at the remaining answer choices before moving on.

Brainstorm

If you get stuck on a difficult question, spend a few seconds quickly brainstorming. Run through the complete list of possible answer choices. Look at each choice and ask yourself, "Could this answer the question satisfactorily?" Go through each answer choice and consider it independently of the other. By systematically going through all possibilities, you may find something that you would otherwise overlook. Remember that when you get stuck, it's important to try to keep moving.

Read Carefully

Understand the problem. Read the question and answer choices carefully. Don't miss the question because you misread the terms. You have plenty of time to read each question thoroughly and make sure you understand what is being asked. Yet a happy medium must be attained, so don't waste too much time. You must read carefully, but efficiently.

Face Value

When in doubt, use common sense. Always accept the situation in the problem at face value. Don't read too much into it. These problems will not require you to make huge leaps of logic. The test writers aren't trying to throw you off with a cheap trick. If you have to go beyond creativity and make a leap of logic in order to have an answer choice answer the question, then you should look at the other answer choices. Don't overcomplicate the problem by creating theoretical relationships or explanations that will warp time or space. These are normal problems rooted in reality. It's just that the applicable relationship or explanation may not be readily apparent and you have to figure things out. Use your common sense to interpret anything that isn't clear.

Prefixes

If you're having trouble with a word in the question or answer choices, try dissecting it. Take advantage of every clue that the word might include. Prefixes and suffixes can be a huge help. Usually they allow you to determine a basic meaning. Pre- means before, post- means after, pro - is positive, de- is negative. From these prefixes and suffixes, you can get an idea of the general meaning of the word and try to put it into context. Beware though of any traps. Just because con is the opposite of pro, doesn't necessarily mean congress is the opposite of progress!

Hedge Phrases

Watch out for critical "hedge" phrases, such as likely, may, can, will often, sometimes, often, almost, mostly, usually, generally, rarely, sometimes. Question writers insert these hedge phrases to cover every possibility. Often an answer choice will be wrong simply because it leaves no room for exception. Avoid answer choices that have definitive words like "exactly," and "always".

Switchback Words

Stay alert for "switchbacks". These are the words and phrases frequently used to alert you to shifts in thought. The most common switchback word is "but". Others include although, however, nevertheless, on the other hand, even though, while, in spite of, despite, regardless of.

- 92 -

New Information

Correct answer choices will rarely have completely new information included. Answer choices typically are straightforward reflections of the material asked about and will directly relate to the question. If a new piece of information is included in an answer choice that doesn't even seem to relate to the topic being asked about, then that answer choice is likely incorrect. All of the information needed to answer the question is usually provided for you, and so you should not have to make guesses that are unsupported or choose answer choices that require unknown information that cannot be reasoned on its own.

Time Management

On technical questions, don't get lost on the technical terms. Don't spend too much time on any one question. If you don't know what a term means, then since you don't have a dictionary, odds are you aren't going to get much further. You should immediately recognize terms as whether or not you know them. If you don't, work with the other clues that you have, the other answer choices and terms provided, but don't waste too much time trying to figure out a difficult term.

Contextual Clues

Look for contextual clues. An answer can be right but not correct. The contextual clues will help you find the answer that is most right and is correct. Understand the context in which a phrase or statement is made. This will help you make important distinctions.

Don't Panic

Panicking will not answer any questions for you. Therefore, it isn't helpful. When you first see the question, if your mind goes blank, take a deep breath. Force yourself to mechanically go through the steps of solving the problem and using the strategies you've learned.

Pace Yourself

Don't get clock fever. It's easy to be overwhelmed when you're looking at a page full of questions, your mind is full of random thoughts and feeling confused, and the clock is ticking down faster than you would like. Calm down and maintain the pace that you have set for yourself. As long as you are on track by monitoring your pace, you are guaranteed to have enough time for yourself. When you get to the last few minutes of the test, it may seem like you won't have enough time left, but if you only have as many questions as you should have left at that point, then you're right on track!

Answer Selection

The best way to pick an answer choice is to eliminate all of those that are wrong, until only one is left and confirm that is the correct answer. Sometimes though, an answer choice may immediately look right. Be careful! Take a second to make sure that the other choices are not equally obvious. Don't make a hasty mistake. There are only two times that you should stop before checking other answers. First is when you are positive that the answer choice you have selected is correct. Second is when time is almost out and you have to make a quick guess!

Check Your Work

Since you will probably not know every term listed and the answer to every question, it is important that you get credit for the ones that you do know. Don't miss any questions through careless mistakes. If at all possible, try to take a second to look back over your answer selection and make sure you've selected the correct answer choice and haven't made a costly careless mistake (such as marking an answer choice that you didn't mean to mark). This quick double check should more than pay for itself in caught mistakes for the time it costs.

Beware of Directly Quoted Answers

Sometimes an answer choice will repeat word for word a portion of the question or reference section. However, beware of such exact duplication – it may be a trap! More than likely, the correct choice will paraphrase or summarize a point, rather than being exactly the same wording.

Slang

Scientific sounding answers are better than slang ones. An answer choice that begins "To compare the outcomes..." is much more likely to be correct than one that begins "Because some people insisted..."

Extreme Statements

Avoid wild answers that throw out highly controversial ideas that are proclaimed as established fact. An answer choice that states the "process should be used in certain situations, if..." is much more likely to be correct than one that states the "process should be discontinued completely." The first is a calm rational statement and doesn't even make a definitive, uncompromising stance, using a hedge word "if" to provide wiggle room, whereas the second choice is a radical idea and far more extreme.

Answer Choice Families

When you have two or more answer choices that are direct opposites or parallels, one of them is usually the correct answer. For instance, if one answer choice states "x increases" and another answer choice states "x decreases" or "y increases," then those two or three answer choices are very similar in construction and fall into the same family of answer choices. A family of answer choices is when two or three answer choices are very similar in construction, and yet often have a directly opposite meaning. Usually the correct answer choice will be in that family of answer choices. The "odd man out" or answer choice that doesn't seem to fit the parallel construction of the other answer choices is more likely to be incorrect.

How to Overcome Test Anxiety

The very nature of tests caters to some level of anxiety, nervousness or tension, just as we feel for any important event that occurs in our lives. A little bit of anxiety or nervousness can be a good thing. It helps us with motivation, and makes achievement just that much sweeter. However, too much anxiety can be a problem; especially if it hinders our ability to function and perform.

"Test anxiety," is the term that refers to the emotional reactions that some test-takers experience when faced with a test or exam. Having a fear of testing and exams is based upon a rational fear, since the test-taker's performance can shape the course of an academic career. Nevertheless, experiencing excessive fear of examinations will only interfere with the test-takers ability to perform, and his/her chances to be successful.

There are a large variety of causes that can contribute to the development and sensation of test anxiety. These include, but are not limited to lack of performance and worrying about issues surrounding the test.

Lack of Preparation

Lack of preparation can be identified by the following behaviors or situations:

Not scheduling enough time to study, and therefore cramming the night before the test or exam
Managing time poorly, to create the sensation that there is not enough time to do everything
Failing to organize the text information in advance, so that the study material consists of the entire text and not simply the pertinent information
Poor overall studying habits

Worrying, on the other hand, can be related to both the test taker, or many other factors around him/her that will be affected by the results of the test. These include worrying about:

Previous performances on similar exams, or exams in general
How friends and other students are achieving
The negative consequences that will result from a poor grade or failure

There are three primary elements to test anxiety. Physical components, which involve the same typical bodily reactions as those to acute anxiety (to be discussed below). Emotional factors have to do with fear or panic. Mental or cognitive issues concerning attention spans and memory abilities.

Physical Signals

There are many different symptoms of test anxiety, and these are not limited to mental and emotional strain. Frequently there are a range of physical signals that will let a test taker know that he/she is suffering from test anxiety. These bodily changes can include the following:

Perspiring
Sweaty palms
Wet, trembling hands
Nausea
Dry mouth
A knot in the stomach
Headache
Faintness
Muscle tension
Aching shoulders, back and neck
Rapid heart beat
Feeling too hot/cold

To recognize the sensation of test anxiety, a test-taker should monitor him/herself for the following sensations:

The physical distress symptoms as listed above
Emotional sensitivity, expressing emotional feelings such as the need to cry or laugh too much, or a sensation of anger or helplessness
A decreased ability to think, causing the test-taker to blank out or have racing thoughts that are hard to organize or control.

Though most students will feel some level of anxiety when faced with a test or exam, the majority can cope with that anxiety and maintain it at a manageable level. However, those who cannot are faced with a very real and very serious condition, which can and should be controlled for the immeasurable benefit of this sufferer.

Naturally, these sensations lead to negative results for the testing experience. The most common effects of test anxiety have to do with nervousness and mental blocking.

Nervousness

Nervousness can appear in several different levels:

The test-taker's difficulty, or even inability to read and understand the questions on the test
The difficulty or inability to organize thoughts to a coherent form
The difficulty or inability to recall key words and concepts relating to the testing questions (especially essays)
The receipt of poor grades on a test, though the test material was well known by the test taker

Conversely, a person may also experience mental blocking, which involves:

Blanking out on test questions
Only remembering the correct answers to the questions when the test has already finished.

Fortunately for test anxiety sufferers, beating these feelings, to a large degree, has to do with proper preparation. When a test taker has a feeling of preparedness, then anxiety will be dramatically lessened.

The first step to resolving anxiety issues is to distinguish which of the two types of anxiety are being suffered. If the anxiety is a direct result of a lack of preparation, this should be considered a normal reaction, and the anxiety level (as opposed to the test results) shouldn't be anything to worry about. However, if, when adequately prepared, the test-taker still panics, blanks out, or seems to overreact, this is not a fully rational reaction. While this can be considered normal too, there are many ways to combat and overcome these effects.

Remember that anxiety cannot be entirely eliminated, however, there are ways to minimize it, to make the anxiety easier to manage. Preparation is one of the best ways to minimize test anxiety. Therefore the following techniques are wise in order to best fight off any anxiety that may want to build.

To begin with, try to avoid cramming before a test, whenever it is possible. By trying to memorize an entire term's worth of information in one day, you'll be shocking your system, and not giving yourself a very good chance to absorb the information. This is an easy path to anxiety, so for those who suffer from test anxiety, cramming should not even be considered an option.

Instead of cramming, work throughout the semester to combine all of the material which is presented throughout the semester, and work on it gradually as the course goes by, making sure to master the main concepts first, leaving minor details for a week or so before the test.

To study for the upcoming exam, be sure to pose questions that may be on the examination, to gauge the ability to answer them by integrating the ideas from your texts, notes and lectures, as well as any supplementary readings.

If it is truly impossible to cover all of the information that was covered in that particular term, concentrate on the most important portions, that can be covered very well. Learn these concepts as best as possible, so that when the test comes, a goal can be made to use these concepts as presentations of your knowledge.

In addition to study habits, changes in attitude are critical to beating a struggle with test anxiety. In fact, an improvement of the perspective over the entire test-taking experience can actually help a test taker to enjoy studying and therefore improve the overall experience. Be certain not to overemphasize the significance of the grade - know that the result of the test is neither a reflection of self worth, nor is it a measure of intelligence; one grade will not predict a person's future success.

To improve an overall testing outlook, the following steps should be tried:

Keeping in mind that the most reasonable expectation for taking a test is to expect to try to demonstrate as much of what you know as you possibly can.
Reminding ourselves that a test is only one test; this is not the only one, and there will be others.
The thought of thinking of oneself in an irrational, all-or-nothing term should be avoided at all costs.
A reward should be designated for after the test, so there's something to look forward to. Whether it be going to a movie, going out to eat, or simply visiting friends, schedule it in advance, and do it no matter what result is expected on the exam.

Test-takers should also keep in mind that the basics are some of the most important things, even beyond anti-anxiety techniques and studying. Never neglect the basic social, emotional and biological needs, in order to try to absorb information. In order to best achieve, these three factors must be held as just as important as the studying itself.

Study Steps

Remember the following important steps for studying:

Maintain healthy nutrition and exercise habits. Continue both your recreational activities and social pass times. These both contribute to your physical and emotional well being.
Be certain to get a good amount of sleep, especially the night before the test, because when you're overtired you are not able to perform to the best of your best ability.
Keep the studying pace to a moderate level by taking breaks when they are needed, and varying the work whenever possible, to keep the mind fresh instead of getting bored. When enough studying has been done that all the material that can be learned has been learned, and the test taker is prepared for the test, stop studying and do something relaxing such as listening to music, watching a movie, or taking a warm bubble bath.

There are also many other techniques to minimize the uneasiness or apprehension that is experienced along with test anxiety before, during, or even after the examination. In fact, there are a great deal of things that can be done to stop anxiety from interfering with lifestyle and performance. Again, remember that anxiety will not be eliminated entirely, and it shouldn't be. Otherwise that "up" feeling for exams would not exist, and most of us depend on that sensation to perform better than usual. However, this anxiety has to be at a level that is manageable.

Of course, as we have just discussed, being prepared for the exam is half the battle right away. Attending all classes, finding out what knowledge will be expected on the exam, and knowing the exam schedules are easy steps to lowering anxiety. Keeping up with work will remove the need to cram, and efficient study habits will eliminate wasted time. Studying should be done in an ideal location for concentration, so that it is simple to become interested in the material and give it complete attention. A method such as SQ3R (Survey, Question, Read, Recite, Review) is a wonderful key to follow to make sure that the study habits are as effective as possible, especially in the case of learning from a textbook. Flashcards are great techniques for memorization. Learning to take good

- 98 -

notes will mean that notes will be full of useful information, so that less sifting will need to be done to seek out what is pertinent for studying. Reviewing notes after class and then again on occasion will keep the information fresh in the mind. From notes that have been taken summary sheets and outlines can be made for simpler reviewing.

A study group can also be a very motivational and helpful place to study, as there will be a sharing of ideas, all of the minds can work together, to make sure that everyone understands, and the studying will be made more interesting because it will be a social occasion.

Basically, though, as long as the test-taker remains organized and self confident, with efficient study habits, less time will need to be spent studying, and higher grades will be achieved.

To become self confident, there are many useful steps. The first of these is "self talk." It has been shown through extensive research, that self-talk for students who suffer from test anxiety, should be well monitored, in order to make sure that it contributes to self confidence as opposed to sinking the student. Frequently the self talk of test-anxious students is negative or self-defeating, thinking that everyone else is smarter and faster, that they always mess up, and that if they don't do well, they'll fail the entire course. It is important to decreasing anxiety that awareness is made of self talk. Try writing any negative self thoughts and then disputing them with a positive statement instead. Begin self-encouragement as though it was a friend speaking. Repeat positive statements to help reprogram the mind to believing in successes instead of failures.

Helpful Techniques

Other extremely helpful techniques include:

Self-visualization of doing well and reaching goals
While aiming for an "A" level of understanding, don't try to "overprotect" by setting your expectations lower. This will only convince the mind to stop studying in order to meet the lower expectations.
Don't make comparisons with the results or habits of other students. These are individual factors, and different things work for different people, causing different results.
Strive to become an expert in learning what works well, and what can be done in order to improve. Consider collecting this data in a journal.
Create rewards for after studying instead of doing things before studying that will only turn into avoidance behaviors.
Make a practice of relaxing - by using methods such as progressive relaxation, self-hypnosis, guided imagery, etc - in order to make relaxation an automatic sensation.
Work on creating a state of relaxed concentration so that concentrating will take on the focus of the mind, so that none will be wasted on worrying.
Take good care of the physical self by eating well and getting enough sleep.
Plan in time for exercise and stick to this plan.

Beyond these techniques, there are other methods to be used before, during and after the test that will help the test-taker perform well in addition to overcoming anxiety.

Before the exam comes the academic preparation. This involves establishing a study schedule and beginning at least one week before the actual date of the test. By doing this, the anxiety of not having enough time to study for the test will be automatically eliminated. Moreover, this will make the studying a much more effective experience, ensuring that the learning will be an easier process. This relieves much undue pressure on the test-taker.

Summary sheets, note cards, and flash cards with the main concepts and examples of these main concepts should be prepared in advance of the actual studying time. A topic should never be eliminated from this process. By omitting a topic because it isn't expected to be on the test is only setting up the test-taker for anxiety should it actually appear on the exam. Utilize the course syllabus for laying out the topics that should be studied. Carefully go over the notes that were made in class, paying special attention to any of the issues that the professor took special care to emphasize while lecturing in class. In the textbooks, use the chapter review, or if possible, the chapter tests, to begin your review.

It may even be possible to ask the instructor what information will be covered on the exam, or what the format of the exam will be (for example, multiple choice, essay, free form, true-false). Additionally, see if it is possible to find out how many questions will be on the test. If a review sheet or sample test has been offered by the professor, make good use of it, above anything else, for the preparation for the test. Another great resource for getting to know the examination is reviewing tests from previous semesters. Use these tests to review, and aim to achieve a 100% score on each of the possible topics. With a few exceptions, the goal that you set for yourself is the highest one that you will reach.

Take all of the questions that were assigned as homework, and rework them to any other possible course material. The more problems reworked, the more skill and confidence will form as a result. When forming the solution to a problem, write out each of the steps. Don't simply do head work. By doing as many steps on paper as possible, much clarification and therefore confidence will be formed. Do this with as many homework problems as possible, before checking the answers. By checking the answer after each problem, a reinforcement will exist, that will not be on the exam. Study situations should be as exam-like as possible, to prime the test-taker's system for the experience. By waiting to check the answers at the end, a psychological advantage will be formed, to decrease the stress factor.

Another fantastic reason for not cramming is the avoidance of confusion in concepts, especially when it comes to mathematics. 8-10 hours of study will become one hundred percent more effective if it is spread out over a week or at least several days, instead of doing it all in one sitting. Recognize that the human brain requires time in order to assimilate new material, so frequent breaks and a span of study time over several days will be much more beneficial.

Additionally, don't study right up until the point of the exam. Studying should stop a minimum of one hour before the exam begins. This allows the brain to rest and put things in their proper order. This will also provide the time to become as relaxed as possible when going into the examination room. The test-taker will also have time to eat well and eat sensibly. Know that the brain needs food as much as the rest of the

- 100 -

Copyright © Mometrix Media. You have been licensed one copy of this document for personal use only. Any other reproduction or redistribution is strictly prohibited. All rights reserved.

body. With enough food and enough sleep, as well as a relaxed attitude, the body and the mind are primed for success.

Avoid any anxious classmates who are talking about the exam. These students only spread anxiety, and are not worth sharing the anxious sentimentalities.

Before the test also involves creating a positive attitude, so mental preparation should also be a point of concentration. There are many keys to creating a positive attitude. Should fears become rushing in, make a visualization of taking the exam, doing well, and seeing an A written on the paper. Write out a list of affirmations that will bring a feeling of confidence, such as "I am doing well in my English class," "I studied well and know my material," "I enjoy this class." Even if the affirmations aren't believed at first, it sends a positive message to the subconscious which will result in an alteration of the overall belief system, which is the system that creates reality.

If a sensation of panic begins, work with the fear and imagine the very worst! Work through the entire scenario of not passing the test, failing the entire course, and dropping out of school, followed by not getting a job, and pushing a shopping cart through the dark alley where you'll live. This will place things into perspective! Then, practice deep breathing and create a visualization of the opposite situation - achieving an "A" on the exam, passing the entire course, receiving the degree at a graduation ceremony.

On the day of the test, there are many things to be done to ensure the best results, as well as the most calm outlook. The following stages are suggested in order to maximize test-taking potential:

Begin the examination day with a moderate breakfast, and avoid any coffee or beverages with caffeine if the test taker is prone to jitters. Even people who are used to managing caffeine can feel jittery or light-headed when it is taken on a test day.
Attempt to do something that is relaxing before the examination begins. As last minute cramming clouds the mastering of overall concepts, it is better to use this time to create a calming outlook.
Be certain to arrive at the test location well in advance, in order to provide time to select a location that is away from doors, windows and other distractions, as well as giving enough time to relax before the test begins.
Keep away from anxiety generating classmates who will upset the sensation of stability and relaxation that is being attempted before the exam.
Should the waiting period before the exam begins cause anxiety, create a self-distraction by reading a light magazine or something else that is relaxing and simple.

During the exam itself, read the entire exam from beginning to end, and find out how much time should be allotted to each individual problem. Once writing the exam, should more time be taken for a problem, it should be abandoned, in order to begin another problem. If there is time at the end, the unfinished problem can always be returned to and completed.

Read the instructions very carefully - twice - so that unpleasant surprises won't follow during or after the exam has ended.

When writing the exam, pretend that the situation is actually simply the completion of homework within a library, or at home. This will assist in forming a relaxed atmosphere, and will allow the brain extra focus for the complex thinking function.

Begin the exam with all of the questions with which the most confidence is felt. This will build the confidence level regarding the entire exam and will begin a quality momentum. This will also create encouragement for trying the problems where uncertainty resides.

Going with the "gut instinct" is always the way to go when solving a problem. Second guessing should be avoided at all costs. Have confidence in the ability to do well.

For essay questions, create an outline in advance that will keep the mind organized and make certain that all of the points are remembered. For multiple choice, read every answer, even if the correct one has been spotted - a better one may exist.

Continue at a pace that is reasonable and not rushed, in order to be able to work carefully. Provide enough time to go over the answers at the end, to check for small errors that can be corrected.

Should a feeling of panic begin, breathe deeply, and think of the feeling of the body releasing sand through its pores. Visualize a calm, peaceful place, and include all of the sights, sounds and sensations of this image. Continue the deep breathing, and take a few minutes to continue this with closed eyes. When all is well again, return to the test.

If a "blanking" occurs for a certain question, skip it and move on to the next question. There will be time to return to the other question later. Get everything done that can be done, first, to guarantee all the grades that can be compiled, and to build all of the confidence possible. Then return to the weaker questions to build the marks from there.

Remember, one's own reality can be created, so as long as the belief is there, success will follow. And remember: anxiety can happen later, right now, there's an exam to be written!

After the examination is complete, whether there is a feeling for a good grade or a bad grade, don't dwell on the exam, and be certain to follow through on the reward that was promised...and enjoy it! Don't dwell on any mistakes that have been made, as there is nothing that can be done at this point anyway.

Additionally, don't begin to study for the next test right away. Do something relaxing for a while, and let the mind relax and prepare itself to begin absorbing information again.

From the results of the exam - both the grade and the entire experience, be certain to learn from what has gone on. Perfect studying habits and work some more on confidence in order to make the next examination experience even better than the last one.

Learn to avoid places where openings occurred for laziness, procrastination and day dreaming.

Use the time between this exam and the next one to better learn to relax, even learning to relax on cue, so that any anxiety can be controlled during the next exam. Learn how to relax the body. Slouch in your chair if that helps. Tighten and then relax all of the different muscle groups, one group at a time, beginning with the feet and then working all the way up to the neck and face. This will ultimately relax the muscles more than they were to begin with. Learn how to breathe deeply and comfortably, and focus on this breathing going in and out as a relaxing thought. With every exhale, repeat the word "relax."

As common as test anxiety is, it is very possible to overcome it. Make yourself one of the test-takers who overcome this frustrating hindrance.

Additional Bonus Material

Due to our efforts to try to keep this book to a manageable length, we've created a link that will give you access to all of your additional bonus material.

Please visit http://www.mometrix.com/bonus948/staareoceng1 to access the information.